——————— *Praise for* ———————
PLEASE DON'T SAY YOU'RE SORRY

"In *Please Don't Say You're Sorry*, Nicole Sodoma shows us that marital struggles, separation, and divorce do not need to be taboo. Quite the opposite, in fact. Sodoma exhibits the experience, humanity, and legal insights that show us how the most tumultuous times can empower great personal choice. Realistic and raw, funny and frank, this book is must-read for anyone trying to find a way to stay in or move past their marriage."

—SONIA CHOQUETTE, Globally Renowned
Spiritual Teacher and 27x *New York Times*
or International Best-selling Author

"Nicole offers a refreshing mix of hope, straight talk, and battle-tested experience. Her compassion for the reader comes through with heart and valuable insights."

— CHRIS JARVIS, Best-selling Financial Author,
Creator of the Go Wild Assessment,
and Entrepreneur Coach

"A thoughtful guide to getting through divorce with the least amount of stress and emotional pain."

—STACY D. PHILLIPS, ESQ., Partner at BLANK ROME
and Author of *Divorce: It's All About Control;*
How to Win the Emotional, Psychological and Legal Wars

"It's about time we pull back the dark velvet curtain that is the delicacy of divorce. *Please Don't Say You're Sorry* is a conversational companion, full of heart and empathy, plus facts from an expert to help you feel a little less alone in this abyss. Page after page you feel that Nicole Sodoma is able to meet you where you are at and help reframe the relationship to yourself as you un-relationship to another. I'm definitely *not* sorry I read this book. And you won't be either."

—ABIGAIL SPENCER, Actress, Writer, and Producer

"*Please Don't Say You're Sorry* is a realistic and straightforward book that helps prepare people for a good divorce or save a good marriage. For anyone looking for an approachable resource, I highly recommend this book."

—ELIZABETH EARNSHAW, LMFT,
Relationship Expert, Founder of @lizlistens,
and Author of *I Want This to Work*

PLEASE DON'T SAY YOU'RE SORRY

AN EMPOWERING PERSPECTIVE ON MARRIAGE, SEPARATION,
AND DIVORCE FROM A MARRIAGE-LOVING DIVORCE ATTORNEY

NICOLE SODOMA

with JOSCELYN DUFFY

Forefront
BOOKS

PLEASE DON'T SAY YOU'RE SORRY: *An Empowering Perspective on Marriage, Separation, and Divorce from a Marriage-Loving Divorce Attorney*

Published by Forefront Books.

Cover Design by Bruce Gore, Gore Studio, Inc.
Interior Design by Mary Susan Oleson, BLU Design Concepts

ISBN: 978-1-63763-080-8 print
ISBN: 978-1-63763-081-5 e-book

For my three birds.
May your inner compass be your guide,
no matter what direction you take.
May you remain open to growing and evolving
with each step of the journey.
And may you always remember
that you are the only one in your way.

CONTENTS

1

It Takes Two to Say "I Do" and One to Say "I Don't"

I DIDN'T KNOW I was going to get divorced. Sometimes women just spontaneously combust.

It all began when I rang in my thirtieth year. I celebrated that milestone birthday by setting a rule for myself as a single professional woman. I decided I would accept any dates I was asked to go on during the two weeks that followed to see what might happen. One of those dates was with the man now known as my former husband. He was thirty-six at the time, ambitious, and—dare I say—charming. Our first real date took place in his 1960s white convertible Chevrolet Impala. Dressed in a crisp shirt and sporting a pair of Converse tennis shoes, he took me to a small neighboring town with an old-fashioned drive-in theater. We sat there on the car's cozy red leather seats watching the big screen and eating Thai food. I didn't kiss him on the first date (which I surmised sparked his interest), and I asked a lot of questions about him, which meant he got to talk the whole time.

Two months later, he asked (in an email) if I wanted to move across the country to Seattle, Washington, where a new job awaited him. My narrative created around the move was that it would be good for "us"; it would allow us to grow together. Despite being nervous and a bit numb, the fantastical idea of marriage and commitment singlehandedly led me to leave behind my network of friends and family in Charlotte, North Carolina, and head west. Was I crazy? I hadn't even introduced my knight to my friends before galloping away on his white horse!

The truth about the not-so-beneficial nature of leaving everything I knew behind was somehow lost in the whirlwind. The story I told myself made friends with my lingering fear that romance might not triumph over what experience had taught me about relationships. My parents' divorce had made a huge impact on my childhood, scarring me with abandonment issues. Yet when faced with the prospect of this new adventure of the heart, I seemed to forget all about that. What I should have been doing was revisiting those fears and pumping the brakes. Instead, I propelled us forward like a sports car in high gear, making checklists, sourcing relocation companies, and securing new housing. Then came the decision to get married.

From the moment my former husband (herein known as Mr. Former, or M.F. for short) proposed to me, there were signs I ignored. And I mean actual signs. We were overlooking a waterfall when he popped the question, and if the steep, rocky descent before us wasn't enough of a hint about what was to come, I had also walked directly over a yellow post on the path leading there that read CAUTION.

I was thirty-one years old and forty minutes late to our wedding when we tied the knot in Anguilla. Ironically, the letter Mr. Former gave me on our big day said that he had waited a lifetime to find me. *So what harm was there in waiting another forty minutes?* While I believed in forever, it occurred to me that I had never lived anywhere longer than five years. I was scared to death of committing to anything long term. I showed up to the nuptials in tears, terrified of the unknown, having talked myself into getting married. *It is the right time. This is the right person, I think.* My mother had even told me it was the right decision for me. What ultimately got me walking down the sandy aisle was the (il)logical thought that, as a divorce attorney and the child of very divorced parents, I understood divorce, so maybe I didn't have to think about *my* marriage as being forever.

On my special day, I was center stage at the beautiful beach wedding of my dreams. The difference between my fantasy and reality was that absolutely no friends or family were there to share in it. Mr. Former and I "agreed" it would be just us. Of course, one of his best friends couldn't make the reception we were planning to host back home, so he rolled up on the shores of Anguilla and crashed our guestless wedding. As we welcomed our wedding crasher into our fairy tale, I had never felt more alone at an occasion that was supposed to be one of the happiest of my life. As M.F. toasted what I imagined was a glass of expensive liquor with one of his best friends, I sat alone on the bed of my hotel room trying to call home for the much-needed affirmation that everything was going to be okay. Just hours into my marriage, I had already started to question whether I had made the right decision.

We lasted all of fifteen months in Seattle before moving back to Charlotte, and as we edged further away from the honeymoon phase of our relationship, the unpleasant parts began to creep in. Those parts—the ones that are not meant for fairy tales—got shoved way down below the surface, scarring my soul a little more. My panic attacks became increasingly difficult to hide. M.F. called them "meltdowns." However, as it turned out, he was having physical symptoms, too, in the form of chest pains. We should have known then that these were a sign of trouble. The truth is, I should have known then.

LIFE CHANGED US DIFFERENTLY.

I think our marriage worked for thirteen years because, much like our first date, I liked to ask questions and to try to make (keep) him happy. The little rational voice in my head knew that marriage should feel like a warm blanket—stable and comforting. In its embrace we should feel heard, understood, and close while also feeling free, untamed, and unrestricted. That wasn't always the case for us. As we went through life together, we lost jobs and started new ones; lost babies and had babies; lost businesses, sold businesses, and even started businesses. We bought promising houses and we also mourned the loss of family members. Along the way, these giant life events were uniquely received by us. They changed us differently. Although at times it felt like we were really strong—us against the world—our goals and values diverged, taking two vastly different roads. Naturally, I tried to convince myself that this wasn't happening.

I married a man who was career driven and who brimmed with confidence. He was someone I believed could take care of me in all ways. For so long in our marriage, he told me that he would die for me, and he truly meant that he would, *so long as I loved him the way he wanted to be loved and I accepted the way he loved me.* I thought he cared deeply enough to do what I needed—what *we* needed—but that's not how everything played out. It always felt like things had to be *his* way and on *his* time.

Being a litigation attorney meant that I was in the middle of conflict all day, making decisions for everyone else. By the time I got home, I was exhausted and no longer had it in me to fight for what *I* wanted.

With each passing year, I began to forget what it was that I desired or needed. Rarely did I question things or push back because I often felt as though I didn't have the opportunity or energy to do so. Whenever it became decision time, I felt like I had only a small peephole of a window in which to act, and those actions were frequently driven by the force of ultimatums I was never ready for. Communication was sticky. Eventually, I shut down. That's when everything blew up.

IN THE INTERVENING YEARS, I EVOLVED.

No longer codependent and relationship focused, I wanted answers, and I wanted out. I also wanted a moment to speak! And so I found someone to talk to—a therapist (or two). Before our separation, M.F. said that if I ever wanted to go to couple's therapy, it would be the end of our marriage. To him, therapy came just before divorce. I disagreed and went to therapy alone.

Following some insights I had while in the cozy chair at the therapist's office, I took myself on two getaways. The trips were intended as a reprieve from the madness of my marriage. I wanted a week without crying or having intrusive thoughts such as, *If I just hit that tree with my car.* . . . Things had admittedly gotten so bad that I considered causing just enough self-harm to land me in the hospital, surrounded by people who might listen. I longed for someone to take care of me and love me in the way I wanted and needed, maybe just for a week or ten days.

After my second getaway, I came back with the intention of throwing Mr. Former the best fiftieth birthday party ever. I invited his closest friends from all over the country and celebrated in style at a local country club. The next morning a handful of us were to leave for a surprise voyage around the British Virgin Islands aboard a fifty-five-foot private catamaran. When it came time for the big reveal, I pulled up a picture of the boat on my computer screen. The blue sky, bright sun, and sailboat never looked more enticing than on that winter night. M.F. glanced at the image, paused, then told me unequivocally that he didn't want to go because he didn't like the other couples I had invited.

For the first time I chose for me and not for us. I went alone and sailed on a catamaran that was ironically named *No Regrets*. Going alone was the bravest thing I had done in our marriage. To fight with Mr. Former over that topic, or any other topic, was the equivalent of poking an angry bear. My attempted rejuvenation through two getaways had failed and the trauma started resurfacing. It didn't look as if there would be an end to the craziness. I didn't know how to communicate effectively with Mr. Former. All I really wanted was for him to take care of himself and find happiness. I went sailing, he finally agreed to counseling, and in time we ended up divorced.

Two to Tango, One to Trot

In my law practice, I had seen divorce many, many times over. But to unexpectedly experience it myself was a whole different ballgame. There's no denying that divorce sucks. You've invested years in a relationship. You've entered into life, business, and—in many cases—parenthood with your partner. Then one day you wake up . . . or they wake up. The hard truth of the dissolution of a marriage is that, while it takes two to say "I do," it takes only one to say "I don't."

It can be incredibly frustrating to think that *one* person has the right to end a marriage that *two* people are in, whether they cheated on you or you were doing the cheating, or whether you are being left or are the one doing the leaving. On that fateful day when one person says "I don't," the other person is almost always left feeling blindsided. My ex-husband still hates me for what I believe to be forcing a choice on him that he didn't want. (And to this day, he seems to find great joy in reminding me of how I alone destroyed him and our three boys.) I left the marriage feeling attacked, hurt, bruised, frustrated, and scared. The giant finger of blame became permanently pointed at me. Although I wasn't angry, I was exhausted.

Divorce is sometimes seen as the easy way out—a get-out-of-jail-free card. But it is most definitely not free (or even cheap). It costs both parties a lot, and the milling of forest trees to cover the legal paperwork costs the earth too. Trust me, divorce is not a hall pass. While it can feel like freedom to some, it can feel like death to others. Either way, it inevitably comes rushing upstream carrying a containership of grief and guilt. It's like a bad dream, even when you didn't realize you were asleep.

It Takes Two to Say "I Do" and One to Say "I Don't"

YOU CONTROL YOU
AND ONLY YOU.

If you haven't considered the unintended conse-quences divorce will have on you, your spouse, your kids, your friends, and your community, then buckle up. It will indeed have an impact. But remember throughout the ordeal that *you control you and only you*, not everyone else who will become involved.

You should also note that if you choose to divorce, the experience can and will change you, but it doesn't have to define you. You get to choose which decision is best for you and how your story plays out from there.

As a divorce attorney for more than two decades, I have seen and heard it all. Almost nothing surprises me. Because of my unique perspective, family and friends often ask me to share what I've learned . . . or to simply answer their bold questions: *Who do you think will be next? Did you hear that so-and-so is sleeping with so-and-so? Do you think their marriage will make it? Do you think he cheated on him?* Or, further from home, *What happened with [insert celeb-rity name here]?*

Such speculations aside, I attempt to answer

your many questions about divorce in this book, drawing from my vast library of wild and crazy stories, which I've gathered while growing up in a blended family of divorced parents, enduring my own divorce, and representing clients who have experienced every circumstance imaginable (and a few that you wouldn't imagine possible). Despite what you may think about divorce attorneys or the title of this book, I'm not a fan of divorce. I believe that it is possible to be tough, to take control of your happiness, and to still like (or love) the idea of marriage.

Divorce isn't always the right path. Maybe I'm too simple or I'm making it seem too straightforward, but to me, divorce is about *choice*. When I think about how much my perspective on divorce has changed since going through it myself, I realize that my views have really evolved. I see divorce as the experience of knowing where you are and where you want to go, then making the necessary choices to get there. *Choice is the only thing you can control.*

You are likely reading this book because you ignored your gut at some point and now you are faced with a similar choice: find a way to make your marriage work or find a way out that won't destroy you. You've lost track of just how many voices are currently holding boardroom-level discussions in your head. If you choose divorce, you'll be confronted with more resolution options than you typically face on New Year's Eve (all weightier than your vow to diet starting January 1). The journey can be wholly overwhelming and emotionally exhausting; however, it doesn't have to be the worst thing that's ever happened to you!

This book is about looking at the separation and divorce process differently, through a unique lens and with a new perspective. It's about keeping afloat in the choppy waters of separation or divorce, but it's also a book about how to stay married if that is what is right for you.

It takes courage to figure out what you want, especially when the decisions are being made by or with someone else. As you work on finding a path forward, I'll offer insightful tidbits (read: antidotes for sleepless nights) and a heaping spoonful of empowerment. Of course, you'll get a good dose of humor, too, because those voices in your head need a laugh or two right now!

Inside these pages are tales from and lessons learned during my personal and professional experiences with divorce. Whether you are looking for advice on how to better your marriage, are considering separation, or find yourself already knee-deep in divorce, this book has something for you. This, however, will not be a body of work that glorifies divorce because I've seen it from every angle and I will be very straight with you. In addition to exposing the realities of relationships, I will offer some empowering principles to help you live and sustain a happy, *real* marriage, and I explore how to know when that's just not possible (and what to realistically expect from there). From hard truths about communication, the popularity of seeking sole custody, and the harsh realities of court proceedings, we'll cover it all, without the heavy details that are likely to overwhelm you. In each chapter, you'll find a set of "Tough Questions." Focus on these. Use them. They will help you get the answers and direction you need. In every chapter you will also find a section of practical resources and tips called "Technically Speaking," because I personally know how much of a difference a helping hand (from a divorce attorney) can make.

TODAY IS THE FIRST DAY OF THE REST OF YOUR LIFE.

It Takes Two to Say "I Do" and One to Say "I Don't"

Choice is the reason this book exists. I've had to make my own choice. I've also been privy to the choices of many others because of the nature of my work. And I want you to know that you are not alone in the moments when you are trying to make those seemingly impossible decisions for yourself. You define you, and the only question remaining after that is, *Where will you go from there?* Believe me when I tell you that today is the first day of the rest of your life, and now is your time. You get to choose if you want a new beginning, whether you decide to stay in your marriage or move beyond it. On the flip side, you also get to choose how you respond to someone else's decision even if you didn't see it coming. Your decision and/or response may change the lives of many, most notably your own. But don't worry—things are looking up because you've now got a badass, no-holds-barred divorce attorney by your side.

2

Please Don't Say You're Sorry

IN MATTERS OF separation and divorce, you can expect sympathy from your sidekicks. However, if you are the one expressing sympathy to your pal who separated or divorced, don't offer such a big wad of it that it will stick with them like a bad case of bubblegum to the shoe, weighing them down with every step. (On rare occasions, large amounts of bubblegum have their use, as I'll explain in a bit.)

A decade into my family law career, a client came to the firm wanting to fight for custody of his son. Mr. Out of State and his then ex-wife were married for a decade in one State, moved to another State for two years, separated just after the birth of their only son, and then divorced. They agreed to joint legal custody; however, the permanent custody order issued by the Court indicated that his ex-wife had primary custody and he had secondary custody. While they were to make major decisions about their son together, she had the final say (which, by the way, really isn't joint legal custody). A year later, a lawsuit was filed and a motion was made to modify the custody terms. After his ex-wife remarried, moved to another State, and got pregnant with another child, she started denying Mr. Out of State access to their son. She wanted full custody, and he wanted more time.

Although Mr. Out of State was a busy entrepreneur and business owner fighting a legal battle across State lines, he was willing to do whatever it took to see his son. Unfortunately, during a temporary hearing, there were allegations that he had abused drugs and had not properly submitted himself for hair follicle tests as required by the Court. Even though you're supposed to be innocent until proven guilty in a criminal court, things tend to work differently in family court. At the most basic levels, you have to show the Court that you are capable, safe, and acting in the best interests of your child. Because of the allegations made, the judge erred on the side of caution, issuing a temporary order that granted my client only supervised visits with his son. However, the judge also made it very clear that if Mr. Out of State could prove he was clean, she would give him an opportunity for shared custody and more time with his son.

My job was to help Mr. Out of State make the judge's promise a reality. We knew that the drug allegations were false, but there would inevitably be plenty of bad or exaggerated stories told about him in the courtroom. I wanted to prove that he was a good person and a good father. The Court needed to see the things he and his son loved to do together. Their relationship was strong and steady. I wanted him to feel like he controlled his case and was not a victim.

INSTEAD OF GOING ON THE DEFENSIVE, CHOOSE TO BE THE OFFENSE ON THE PLAYING FIELD.

The alternative to saying, "F* you, I don't have a drug problem," was to go on the offensive and exemplify just how bogus the drug claim was. And so, every single week I sent Mr. Out of State to a local facility for a drug screen. Over eleven months, we quietly and intentionally accumulated more than 180 (negative) test results. By the time the trial began, we had boxes full of test results. (A small forest of trees was sacrificed to provide all the paper they were written on!) I walked into the courtroom with those boxes in tow. I also came bearing a giant fishbowl of individually wrapped pieces of bubblegum.

Every morning of the four-day trial, I would start off by (quite obviously) breaking into a fresh piece of that luscious gum. I'd offer a piece to the court clerk, opposing counsel, my paralegal, and my client. When it came time for my closing argument, I pointed out that the fishbowl contained 180 pieces of gum on day one of the trial and that we had hardly made a dent in the bowl after four days of testimony. One hundred eighty was the number of days my client took time off work, drove thirty minutes each way, and paid $120 per drug test to show the Court he was committed to his son. It was exactly the kind of evidence I knew would stick in Court (pardon the pun). On the big screen, I posted a written version of what the judge essentially told my client at his initial hearing: If you can prove you are clean, I will give you an opportunity. The judge decided that she owed it to him to give him what he gave her: the assurance he was not what others said he was.[1] My client was granted more time with his son.

A Symphony of Sympathies

The dissolution of a marriage or relationship of any kind is like the ocean: you can't stop the waves from coming. All you can do is grab your surfboard and figure out how to not drown. It's important to realize that you *always* have a choice in how you act, react, and reach forward. You can swim or not swim. You can surf in the areas marked DANGEROUS, or you can stay away. You can either wait for the right wave or take the first one you see. No one said that knowing what to do is going to be easy or obvious, but you get to ride however you decide. It's all about having the right information so you can make the best choice for you.

Mr. Out of State spent five years going through divorce and in litigation in different cities and States. While fighting for custody, he said he had no idea how much "emotional endurance" would be required of him during his case. He was exhausted. Anyone could have said they were sorry for what he was going through, placing him in the victim box and causing him to lose sight of what he wanted and was battling for. Instead, he chose to surround himself with people who were his supporters—those who encouraged his happiness, who knew his intentions were solid, and who stood by him through the most challenging times. He was willing to fight for what he felt was best for his son and, ultimately, for himself. He kept his eyes on the ocean, prepared for the best wave, and rode with intention. In the end, he didn't have to say he was sorry for something he didn't do or something he wasn't.

THE WORDS "I'M SORRY" ARE A SURE-FIRE WAY TO SEND YOU STRAIGHT BACK TO A PLACE OF GUILT AND SORROW.

Why it is that people say "I'm sorry" when we divorce? "Sorry," a word used to express empathy for someone's misfortune, hardly seems fitting for a circumstance where you are choosing to do what is in the best interest of your happiness (and perhaps that of your partner and children too). When Mr. Former and I split, I believed the damage was irreparable. The "I'm sorry" messages rolled in like an annoyingly leaky faucet I couldn't put a wrench to. Through the cacophony of sympathies, all I wanted to tell everyone was, *Please don't say you're sorry!* The tears I had fought so hard to hold back streamed down my face at night when no one was watching. Hearing the words "I'm sorry" became a sure-fire way to trigger deep feelings of guilt and sorrow. No passing Go. No collecting $200. My thoughts would swirl with apologies I should make, remorse I felt, and then, ultimately, the soul-crushing shame I endured. I would not be a victim, but the incoming stream of "sorries" sure had me feeling like one. I longed to bottle up every single apology and give it with my whole heart to my three boys. I was not the badass tough cookie I thought I was, but I was always their mom, no matter what. In the end, I was sorry too.

After the initial separation, the roller coaster of grief and freedom I had been riding began to steady. I attended an event at a local restaurant in celebration of a long-time friend's partnership at her financial advisory firm. There I ran into an old colleague, and we shared some prosecco (a little bubbly at the end of a day makes me feel like I am celebrating, no matter what kind of day it was). As we caught up on old gossip, I said, "You heard, right?" She replied, "Heard what?" I told her Mr. Former and I had split. Then she said it. The dreaded leaky-faucet drip I couldn't fix grew louder: "I am so sorry."

Those words made me cringe every single time, reverberating in my ears like my aunt's high-pitched cackle, a loud crack of thunder waking me from a sound sleep, or the worst heavy metal song I could think of from the 1980s. I flipped. *What are all these people sorry for?!* Busting out in uncomfortable laughter, I said, "Sorry for what? You don't know where I have been or whether I chose to be where I am now. You don't know if I woke up one morning and ruined someone's life or if I escaped a lifetime of unhappiness."

I'd hit my breaking point. Amid all the labels, grief, loss, change, and fear, the last thing I wanted or needed was another woe-is-me conversation. Endlessly explaining the how and why of my seemingly perfect marriage's end had weighed me down long enough. I had also spent a lifetime watching people apologize for things they may or may not have been sorry for. At least when we marry and people say "Congratulations," we are being wished something happy. Though, ironically, we are heading into a partnership and life that's going to require growth, work, and even hardship! And for that, I'm sorry.

Challenging the State of Sorry

What are you really sorry for? Say that! *Sorry for a love lost. Sorry that you are sad. Sorry for your grief.* Please don't leave us hanging. And how about using the word "sorry" in a truly heartfelt way that does not make the hurting party relive the trauma or even feel obliged to forgive you (if you were the person causing the hurt)?

IF YOU ARE GOING TO SAY YOU ARE SORRY, AT LEAST FINISH THE SENTENCE!

Despite hearing "sorry" incessantly during my own divorce, I never used the word during a divorce consultation with a client before (or since) then. Why? Because I didn't know what stage of the emotional process they were in or what was going on in their relationship. Were they the one leaving or being left? My questions and sympathies set the tone for our meeting, and I never wanted a client to start off feeling like a victim. Instead, I would tell them that I was sorry they were there in that chair . . . but that there had also been a lot of other people in that chair! Whatever their story, we had information to gather and choices to make, and in our work together, we would *never* be sorry.

But after bubbling over at my friend's partnership party, it became clear to me that I had to do more than that to actively challenge the state of sorry. I set out on a mission to find a less knee-jerk divorce response. I wanted one filled with greater empowerment and maybe, just maybe, a smidgen of hope, support, and optimism. Like, how about saying "I'm here" instead of "I'm sorry"?

- I'm here for you.
- I'm here if you need me.
- I'm here if you want someone to listen.
- I'm here to talk through things.
- I'm here with (a lot of) wine, or I'm here with dinner (preferably in that order).
- I'm here, and I've got you.

Even just, "I'm picking you up on Sunday and taking you to a trashy movie, a football game, or to binge on Netflix documentaries." And while you're at it, why not throw in an "I understand" or "Thanks for sharing" or "Thank you for your courage"? These responses are healthy and might even be welcomed.

NEVER APOLOGIZE FOR PLACING YOUR HAPPINESS FIRST.

"Sorry" doesn't fit all circumstances because often, there is nothing to be sorry about! Divorce may not be a bad thing when it is the right decision for you. Never apologize for placing your happiness first and don't put up with being swallowed whole by a swell of sorries coming your way. If you're on the receiving end, change the narrative and the state of sorry. Instead of saying that you are divorced, you can always simply say, "I am not married." Interestingly, most people will not say they are sorry for that!

The Tough Questions

1. How do you feel when someone says they are sorry for you? Are you willing to change the state of sorry? Is today your day? Is the damage irreparable?

2. If there are allegations against you, are you willing to prove your innocence if you need to? Or are you too stubborn?

3. What are you not telling? What are you afraid of?

Technically Speaking

If you're going to go through separation and divorce, you need to know the lingo. That's why, at the end of the book, you'll find the Glossary of Simplified Legal Speak, where I define legal terms in more human language. Throughout the book, the Technically Speaking sections will also offer helpful tips for journeying through marriage, separation, or divorce. Relevant tips for this chapter are:

• When it comes to gathering supporters,

resources, and healing help, don't start when the trouble starts.

- Throughout your marriage, it is healthy to cultivate a network of good friends. Don't wait until you see the end is near. Of course, like everything else in life, the value of what you put in is likely the value of what you will get out. Lean in.

- Identify and discuss the efforts you and your spouse each intend to make to improve your marriage or to move past it.

- Having appeared with some of my favorites (Oprah Winfrey and Anderson Cooper, among others), Steven Stosny, Ph.D., is the founder of CompassionPower and one of my top teacher choices. You might want to check out his books *Empowered Love: Use Your Brain to Be Your Best Self and Create Your Ideal Relationship* and *Soar Above: How to Use the Most Profound Part of Your Brain Under Any Kind of Stress.*

PART ONE

MARRIAGE

THE WORD *YES* IS EXCLAIMED, and visions of a beautiful wedding surrounded by family and friends begin to emerge. She said *yes*! *Yes* to the dress! *Yes* to the big day! We see it on American reality television shows and in ads for wedding planners, vendors, and venues. Regardless of culture, religion, or socio-economic status, marriage is perceived as a celebration of the love two people share. It is, no doubt, a monumental moment in the lives of those saying, "I do." But a wedding ceremony is much more than a celebration of a great romance. The act of getting a marriage license and sharing in a wedding ceremony, whatever that may look like, is the process that creates a legally binding marriage contract.

Most people avoid entering a contract that could have a significant impact on their daily lives without having a full understanding of the agreement's implications or even a sense of how much work will be required of them to maintain it. Whether it's a mortgage agreement, an apartment lease, or an employment contract, they do the work to be sure they comprehend the terms involved. Yet surprisingly, many people tie the knot without appreciating the legal impact and, in some cases, the unintended consequences. What often goes unrealized is how this contract changes the financial and legal interests of each person literally overnight.

Regardless of whether your path leads to a successful or failed marriage, understanding the legal and financial implications is essential from the start. A real marriage is about so much more than companionship, which is often what we celebrate on the big day. Yes, companionship will be paramount when our bodies don't function the way they did in our twenties—and it may be more important than ever during these challenging modern times—but that's not all a marriage requires to be successful.

During thousands of consults with clients, I have heard several common themes repeated regularly: loyalty, trust, maintaining and creating healthy boundaries, speaking openly, standing beside each other in support and in defeat, understanding where you each stand, having chemistry, enjoying intimacy, communicating effectively, and sharing common core values are all equally important in maintaining a union that can stand the test of time. Steven Stosny, Ph.D. describes happiness not as a goal but "a by-product of [a] core value" and also notes that "we have to create value because it doesn't exist in nature." Why? Because the creation of value is the part of anything that increases our sense of self by increasing our motivation to learn, appreciate, grow, improve, connect, or protect.[2] It's all part of an innate drive to create meaning and purpose, and it's the part of marriage we should all be seeking (while understanding the legalities).

3

The People We Marry Are Not the People We Divorce

FOR SO LONG I didn't know what I didn't know. As an engaged thirty-one-year-old divorce lawyer, I remember telling opposing counsel before a trial that I was getting married. She laughed and said, "Nice to see that hope triumphs over our experience in this courtroom." I smiled uncomfortably and began my opening argument, hoping she didn't notice how her words landed with me. I wondered if I was going to be brave enough to show her she was wrong. Could I take things one step further and be the leader of the bold (or the crazy) divorce lawyers who marry without a prenuptial agreement just to prove a point?

In my adolescence, I wanted to be a follower

because I never felt good enough, cool enough, or just plain "enough." Today things are very different. I am relational, candid, and pointed. Don't get me wrong. I still enjoy a good follow from time to time. In those cases, I'll attentively listen, learn, and then try to do it better than they did. I'll prick up my ears to solve problems and to educate and empower others. I don't enjoy hiding behind man-made boundaries. I say what others are thinking, and I am deliberate and intentional with my words (even the inappropriate ones). I believe that challenging what's accepted is how change happens. My disruptive yet approachable leadership style developed over time, despite myself, because sometimes it can feel easier to go with the flow.

As I led triumphantly in business and my community, the hard truth was that for the last years of my marriage, I walked on eggshells, silenced. Only one phrase kept the peace: *Okay, I'm sorry*. When Mr. Former and I weren't arguing, we were masking how we felt—usually with wine, sleep, a Netflix binge, or an endless stream of Pinterest searches. Our determination to distract ourselves became so exhaustive I would joke that he'd soon find the end of the Internet. When there was an attempt at discussion, one thing was certain: there was no talking back or arguing my point of view because it would only increase the conflict and result in my apology. "Don't poke the bear," he would remind me. I was never able to say how I felt, at least not in a way that he could hear. I longed to fight and debate things like "normal" people did. You yell. I yell. We laugh at each other. We make up. Instead, M.F. and I never finished a fight or fully understood both sides of the argument. Where was the woman who challenged the norm? How could I defy stereotypes and be so strong in my leadership outside of our home but so weak in my own marriage?

It had become all too easy to accept my husband's (seeming lack of) belief in me as my truth. When things got dark, he would tell me how *he really felt* and the ugly parts of our marriage would become harder and harder to ignore. He would tell me that I was poor in business and management. "Enjoy running the firm right into the ground," he texted. I wasn't good enough to satisfy him sexually. I didn't prioritize him above my work. He wanted more of everything (three children, several businesses, great community ties, caring friends, and a loving family is not enough for everyone). I was to blame. I never felt enough.

THINGS DON'T FIX THEMSELVES, NOR CAN YOU SINGLE-HANDEDLY FIX THEM.

Why didn't I measure up to M.F.'s standards? It felt as if the man who was supposed to be my biggest supporter was casting doubts on me, amplifying my own insecurities and fears—even on the days when I felt successful, offered gratitude, or shifted the "win" to him to keep us balanced. That was my way of apologizing for not meeting his unmeetable expectations. I was heartbroken to be such a disappointment to him.

Why, for so long, was my happiness conditioned upon his happiness? It probably didn't help that I was simultaneously seeking his approval and affirmation on almost everything. When he told me for the final time, standing in our kitchen, that he resented me and blamed me for how his life had turned out, I knew it was time for me to make a decision. "Okay, I'm sorry," had become my steady, shrink-worthy, unhealthy response pattern—a pattern I was desperate to break. It was time to stop accommodating to avoid a fight. The insecure, approval-seeking partner had to be extricated because things weren't fixing themselves. I couldn't single-handedly fix us.

When I finally woke up and caught a glimpse of sunlight peeking over the brick wall of my fortress, I stood up and said, "I can't do this anymore." Mr. Former seemed wholly blindsided. It was as if he suffered from sudden memory loss, having forgotten all the times he told me that he didn't want to be married to me anymore. For both of us, I made the only big decision I ever made independently in my marriage: to end it.

Why didn't I care enough to stand up and say something sooner? Was it a lack of courage or energy? A survival tactic I was deploying? Was it because of our children? An addiction to the idea of love? Fear that there were no greener pastures beyond this one? Why didn't I advocate for myself the way I do for my clients? If I'd stood up and spoken fiercely for us, would it just have ended our marriage sooner? Or would the crisis have been averted?

For the gift of my three boys, getting married

was the best decision ever. They are the loves of my life. For my relational happiness, however, it was not a good decision. I must say that my Pollyanna perspective on co-parenting prior to my divorce certainly changed post-divorce, as did the counsel I provide my clients, colleagues, and friends. But conditional love was the biggest hurdle I didn't see coming.

CONDITIONAL LOVE WILL ALWAYS HAVE UNINTENTIONAL CONSEQUENCES.

Do you truly know how your partner will respond once you have poured your heart out and shared your resentments? I wildly underestimated the hardship and beatdowns that separation and divorce would pack for me. Were it not for my dreams of change and challenging the norm, I might never have made the decision to leave and put myself in the thick of the opinions that poured out of those leaky faucets I couldn't fix.

There Is No Changing Someone Else

All too often, we are taught to look for Mr. or Mrs. Right. When I married Mr. Former, my mother repeatedly told me that he was the "right one" for me. In her 1996 Jane Pauley interview (I'm dating myself a bit here), Cher said that her mother once told her to "Settle down and marry a rich man." Cher responded, "Mom, I am a rich man." My philosophy is basic: pick your partner because you like them, not because you need them. You should also know up front that what you see in your Mr. or Mrs. Right may not be what you get over time. You change, they change, and not always in the way you dreamed of when you said *yes*.

Changes in a partner can be simple, like going from being a dog lover to a cat lover. But what about the changes that happen as you go from wife to mother or father to grandfather? Or if you make the decision to go from wife to husband or husband to wife in order to become who you always felt you authentically were? What if a change involves discovering a mental or medical condition that requires treatment? What if roles unexpectedly get reversed due to job loss or promotion? How will the relationship handle the financial toll? Can you manage these big life changes and the ways they may change you? Can you compassionately understand the impact on your partner and turn toward them instead of away? These are the questions you should be asking yourself.

There is no such thing as a perfect marriage. Even looking back on your wedding day, there are likely things you would have changed (like maybe not being forty minutes late and perhaps inviting your besties to join in the celebration with you). It's not realistic to expect perfection from your marriage or partner every minute of every day. Recognizing that you control only yourself and that you cannot change someone else will always be one of the biggest and hardest lessons learned in any relationship (and one that comes up in every consult I have with a new client).

As I sit with clients, they will frequently try to predict how their partner is going to respond, as if they are trying to perfect their mind-reading skills. They will often spend more time telling me about someone else's feelings than their own. One of those sets of feelings is within their control, and one is not. As a parent, you can teach your children something, but you can't do it for them. (Granted, in thirty years electric cars may be tying their shoelaces for them. Bye-bye, bunny ears!) As a partner or spouse, you can share your feelings, but you can't make others feel the same way (or telepathically change their minds). As a lawyer, you can present the facts and use your arguments and the case law that supports you, but you can't control the outcome of your case. Judges have bad days too. As an employer, you can create culture, policy, benefits, and opportunity, but you can't force employees to have the same vision, commitment, or work ethic. The moral of the story is that you can always work on you, but you can only *try to inspire* others. People are going to change in the way they want and when *they* want—not in the way you want or when you want—no matter how many hours you put into perfecting your mind-reading and mind-shifting capabilities.

WORKING ON "YOU" AND "US" (AND NOT ON "THEM") IS EVERYTHING.

Globally renowned relational intelligence expert Esther Perel says that when transitioning between stages of a relationship, you enter the doors of "The Great Adaptation." In her work, she talks about how to "stay grounded when the ground is moving." Her advice: "When you have flexibility, you can bend without breaking. . . . Bending is what we are called to do when we can't change our circumstances, when we can only change the way that we react to them." Like the physical stretch that awakens the body, bending gives you greater flexibility, agility, and nimbleness.[3]

You and your spouse can grow and learn together, but you must evolve together, not revolve around each other. Through the divorce or reconciliation process, I have seen this accomplished with help from therapists, clergy, family members, or friends, but rarely is it done alone without these resources. Acknowledging each other's differences along the way is one step in the process, but learning how to adjust, communicate, and find *your way* must be a priority when trying to maintain a successful marriage. When things get rocky, you cannot change your partner; only they can change themselves. You'll need to take a step back and decide if you want to work on yourself and accommodate those who don't want to do the work alongside you.

Take Me Back to When You First Met

During initial consults with clients, I love asking "softball questions." Just like lobbing an easy-to-hit pitch from the baseball mound, I make simple inquiries about their lives and kids. *Where do you live? What holidays are most important to you? What are some of your family traditions? Do you have any pictures of your kids?* (Because I like to see who I'm talking about and, of course, I want to check their phone to make sure they are not recording me. Do not record your lawyer! Privilege only exists between counsel and client; should a recording fall into the wrong hands it will backfire on you.) These softball questions allow me to find a common denominator, among other things I need to know and understand about them. They also put my clients in the driver's seat.

Recently, a client came to me knowing that his divorce was a long time coming. He felt very resolved (as men often do by the time they get to my office for a consultation). To his surprise, I asked him how he and his wife met. There was a pause, as if not expecting such a positive, backward-facing inquiry. Then came the inevitable loss of eye contact and the appearance of a little smirk before he told me about their first encounter. From the beginning of the consult to the end, he smiled every time he shared stories about his wife. He described their relationship as being a happy marriage, until they both realized they could no longer make it work.

On the wall in my gym hangs a sign that reads, "When you want to quit, remember why you started." If you are struggling in your marriage and thinking about getting divorced, ask the questions that help you remember why the relationship began. "Do you remember the first time you met? The first date? Were you ready on time? Do you remember what you wore? Where were you? How were you feeling?" The answers to these questions may be just what you need to hear to pull you back up from the grief. Your relationship has history, and both of you will have versions and favorite moments. Every time you tell a story from your past, the feelings may be enough to help carry you forward in a positive way. Even in the most difficult of divorce cases, finding positivity can help you break through to a resolution.

In any circumstance when a marriage is on the brink of dissolution, or it is already deep in the trenches of coming to a permanent end via divorce,

we are talking about you and another human being
(even if sometimes you question whether your spouse
is still human). Remembering how you met allows
you to take a break from whatever chaos and conflict
you are experiencing. It will also help you warm up
to speaking more openly and vulnerably about where
you stand. That is advice I could have used during all
those years when I remained captive in my fortress of
"Okay, I'm sorry"!

YOUR HAPPINESS IS NOT SOMEONE ELSE'S HAPPINESS.

Let me say that again: your happiness is not
someone else's happiness. What works for your
friend may not work for you. Women, in particular,
tend to condition their own happiness on the happiness of their partner. Learning to be independent
of that behavior can be incredibly difficult. Clearly,
there needs to be some compromise on this concept,
but making yourself happy should be as critical as
ensuring the happiness of your partner. Otherwise,

you can both expect to feel like a hostage held to an emotion that you have absolutely no control over, especially as you evolve, grow, and change from the people you were when you married. When you know more, you'll be better and do better. (Thank you for the continued and beloved wisdom, Maya Angelou.) Work on yourself and remember that there is no sense in trying if you don't give it your all. Do whatever you need to do to resolve or dissolve your relationship in the way that is best for you.

The Tough Questions

1. Do you want to save your marriage?

2. What is your motivation to stay or go?

3. Have you already done everything you can do to rescue your relationship?

4. What would you do if you were not afraid of the confrontation or the consequences?

5. How can you best prepare yourself for having a difficult or even a "care-frontational" conversation with your spouse? Will personal vulnerability get in your way, or will it be your ally?

6. Do you know your core values and feel intentional in your actions and conversations?

7. Why aren't you having the tough conversations? What are you not saying?

Technically Speaking

When it comes to resolving or dissolving your marriage, the first step is to find a process that works for you. There are amazing resources at your fingertips. Here are many things that helped me:

- Go back in time with your memories and through therapy.

- Go forward with coaching and resources.

- Give yourself a day off from thinking about resolution and do something that inspires you. Active meditation created the space in my head to quiet the voices. It is a mediation style practiced through physical activity. It brings such clarity, awareness, and maybe even a restful night of sleep.

- Make a list of your nonnegotiables.

- Make another list of what you would miss or wouldn't miss.

- Consult with a divorce attorney to get a real sense of what the journey will hold.

- Identify your best support system, hopefully one that holds back on judgment, because the stories you tell yourself during the journey of divorce may change over time.

- If you are working on confrontation or how to manage conflict, read from the works of authors such as Eckhart Tolle, Dr. Henry Cloud, Belinda Berman, Sandra Brown, Gloria Steinem, Patricia Evans, Brené Brown, Glennon Doyle (*Untamed*), Melody Beattie (*The Language of Letting Go*), Alexandra H. Solomon (*Loving Bravely*), and others who explore the psychology of self and relationships. The list of authorities in this area is long, but these are a few of my favorites.

4

Find Out What's Up, Long Before Things Go Down

The Girl in the Cowboy Boots

ONE FRIDAY AFTERNOON at 5 o'clock, I was uptown with my sneakers laced, about to start the Truist Corporate Cup 5K to burn off steam after a big week. My phone was tucked in my bra. (Remember the days when phones were too big for an armband and fanny packs were so 1980s?) I was standing at the starting line when my boobs rang. It was my receptionist. She sounded panicked. I asked her what was up and told her I would be out of pocket for a bit because I was about to start a race. She quickly retorted, "Oh no, you're not."

Another attorney from my office jumped on the line and told me to look at the firm's security cameras, which I could access from my phone. I did, and there in our lobby stood a young woman in cowboy boots and a very short skirt. Through the security system and the phone line, I listened to her as she spoke with another attorney in my office. Throughout the exchange I tried to keep pace with the speed of her dialogue (which was arguably much faster than my running pace ever would be). She said that Mr. High Roller (so we'll call him) owed her $7,000 because she'd been his escort for the past week. They had been staying in a fancy hotel, and he was now refusing to pay her. When she shared a detail that only someone who intimately knew this family would know, it was clear she was legit.

The man in question was our client's husband. They were recently separated, and we were working through financial matters. Ms. Cowboy Boots offered to go to court with us the following week if we could get her paid. Obviously, that wasn't legally possible, so instead, I took a screenshot of her on the security camera and told her we'd see what we could do.

On Monday morning, I used the screenshot as evidence that a man who refused to work—and who represented to the Court and to his wife that he had no money to support himself, his family, or his children—had actually been paying $1,000 per night for an escort and living it up with her at a swanky hotel! (The remaining balance was $7,000, and he acknowledged he would eventually pay her.) In a room full of attorneys awaiting the start of their own clients' hearings, I held up the picture of the girl in the cowboy boots standing in our firm's lobby and asked the husband if he recognized the woman. "I bought her those boots!" he said. No hesitation, no remorse. He walked right into it like a rich man prancing into a spa in a big, white, fuzzy bathrobe and slippers. On the bench in front of us, the judge's head literally fell onto her desk before she rolled her eyes and made her ruling.

A LACK OF FINANCIAL AWARENESS IN A MARRIAGE IS NOT AN UNCOMMON SCENARIO.

Finances can be daunting, a platform for potential deceit, and one of the most volatile pieces of a marriage. They are challenging when you know the collective accounts you and your spouse hold, but what if you don't? I assure you that finding yourself financially in the dark is not a unique occurrence, even for this marriage-loving divorce attorney. Many clients will come to our office and sheepishly admit that they know nothing about their finances. They apologize for being one of "those people" who has no clue what they own and then ask how they can find out what they need to know.

Once litigation is filed (either you or your spouse file a legal action requesting a divorce, custody, support, alimony, a division of property, and so on), you can obtain relevant account statements through a subpoena (or at least know if the account exists or existed). But if you don't even know where to send the subpoena, prepare for an expensive and time-consuming process. Is your counsel going to send the subpoena to *every single banking institution*? And what if your pursuit only leads to the discovery of $400 in a single account because the cash has been hidden high in the rafters instead of in a vault? Maybe my example seems far-fetched, but I have seen discoveries of almost one million dollars concealed somewhere in a house and thousands more buried in the yard. Don't dig blindly. It's not easy, nor is it cheap to have a lawyer who bills you hourly go through years of bank statements! Be proactive and find a simple way to figure things out. Have you ever deposited a check at a certain bank, looked at bank statements, noticed money being transferred to or from an account, or seen a return of interest income on a tax filing? Is there a cabinet in your home office where such statements might be kept? Or a desk drawer where they could have been shoved away?

    The challenges you face when demanding to know about your shared finances should have simpler solutions; however, that is not always the case. For those of you feeling lost and overwhelmed by the prospect of having to become a financial sleuth on par with Sherlock Holmes or Nancy Drew, don't give up hope. Sometimes when money matters are in question and you don't feel like you know what you have, all you can do is flaunt your brilliant head of blonde hair and play naïve at a local bank, as I admittedly once had to do.

Asleep Until Shaken Awake

For years I was running a multi-office law firm, but with the exception of my one credit card (which often incurred late fees) and managing my own "blue jeans" checking account, I never paid a personal bill or household expense. Mr. Former took care of all our personal finances. It was clear that, despite all the years of front-line experience with relationships and divorce my career afforded, I still upheld the antiquated practice of being "taken care of" by my husband. In the end, egg was on my face. When we separated, I discovered that my ex had created more banking relationships than I knew about. And there were times when he was making multiple transactions a day between those accounts, in rather significant amounts. It was so complex that no one could follow it—not me and likely not even a judge. (This is a great strategy if your jurisdiction has a busy and time-restricted trial schedule, by the way.)

Determined to find answers and understand whether there were more accounts, I set out on a lunchtime mission one sunny summer afternoon. I fluffed up my mane of long blonde hair and strutted into the local branch office of a large bank. As I walked through the door, a bank associate gave me a welcoming smile and the stage was set. I confidently made my way over and sat in the empty chair across from her, stating in my most naïve voice, "I know we have an account here, but I can't get online. My husband is traveling, and I need to be able to access our account."

"What's your last name and social security number?" she asked me. I gave her Mr. Former's information and my own and nodded confidently as she repeated the numbers back to me. She turned her computer screen in my direction, and I told her which statements to print. I thanked her for being so helpful. The statements showed the account I knew about and a second one that I did not. She told me that the second account had been emptied. My heart sank. I'd had the same experience as so many of my clients. I was too late; the money was gone. Apparently, so was my ability to remember my own advice: the people we marry are not the people we divorce.

M.F. (an alias that now seems as if it could also mean professional "Mover of Funds") may have had good intentions in moving money out of the account, but those intentions had not been disclosed to me. Whenever I have forgetful moments, I typically brush them off with a laugh and tell people that I pay for my blonde hair. But not that day at the bank. Purposefully acting like a stereotypical blonde had served me very well. Had I not Nancy Drewed the heck out of my hunches, the money once in that account would never have been on my radar. And if I had taken my own advice, I would have gotten to the cash, split it, and closed the account myself.

Have the Hard Money Talk

When it was clear that Mr. Former and I were going to start a life together, he handed me a packet of financial documents requiring my input. They asked about my investment styles (i.e., aggressive, moderate, or conservative), when I wanted to retire, how much I wanted to put away in a college fund for the children I had not yet birthed (OMG), and the like. The packet was easily *twenty pages thick*, written in a small font with text covering both the front and back of every page. After taking a long sip of my coffee, I flipped the packet over and wrote in bold letters, *I am not interested, signed Nicole*. I had simply rejected the terms of his financial endearment. He later adjusted his terms by taking over our finances for the duration of our thirteen-year marriage. The moral of the story is don't accept what absolutely won't work for you, but be ready to accept the consequences if you insist on burying your head in the sand.

A LACK OF FINANCIAL INSIGHT CAN DRIVE DISTRUST AND INSTILL A FEAR OF SEPARATION.

More often than not, one person's head is dug deeper than an iPhone in a triple-D cup when it comes to all things finances. And that lack of insight is what ultimately drives distrust and fear of separation. Financial awareness is one of the greatest points of empowerment you can give yourself. Why? Because shit happens. Partners cheat. They can. They might. You may. Or you might not. Whatever the circumstances, your dual-income family may turn into a single-income family without your permission. If you tell your attorney that you don't have access to your partner's phone or that there is a credit card you don't know about, a password you don't have, or a bank account you can't access, then brace yourself for the possibility. Your power lies in tackling the hard money talks with your spouse today.

There are always two or more sides to every story, and as a family law attorney, I've heard nearly every version of every story. Trust me, the question of whether the other person is hiding money (intentionally or unintentionally) is real. The further question of whether only one of you can clean out a joint account is also very real.

Is the juice worth the squeeze? Is the information you are seeking worth knowing? In any marriage, you're going to have to have those come-to-Jesus conversations that will inevitably change the way everything looks. It may be a talk about an old fling, college frat party drama (or trauma), or a misdemeanor from that time you were underage and got busted with a beer in hand. Drs. John and Julie Gottman, forty-year veteran researchers studying what makes relationships work (and founders of the Gottman Institute), surely have a lot to say about this. In fact, they wrote the book on the need for regular conversations about big issues. It's called *Eight Dates: Essential Conversations for a Lifetime of Love*.

Of the hundreds of divorce consultations I've had, financial conflict or hardship tends to be one of the leading issues and one of the hardest conversations to have. Rarely do two people agree to save or spend the same amount. Even if you have no interest in finances, aren't employed, or are the breadwinner, understanding your family's financials has absolutely no downside. As a breadwinner or the person in charge of paying the bills, a tremendous weight falls on you to be sure you are doing it right. As the homemaker, supported spouse, or the one not in charge of the family's financial affairs (but in charge of everything else), you need to be accountable too. Why not get involved and be a part of the conversation? What are you afraid of? Would you rather spend your time worrying or enjoying life?

THE ALARM HAS SOUNDED, NOW RISE 'N SHINE!

You've been forewarned. You can question if your spouse is hiding money later, or you can begin the habit of talking things through now so you know what's up long before things go down. Your power lies in knowing where your money is going, where the passwords are stored, where life insurance policies are held, and what your financial picture will look like when your children are grown. If things have gotten to a point where you're going to go after your spouse, you really should know what you're going after! And for the record, cash cannot be tracked. ATMs can be a divorce lawyer's worst nightmare (you can see the cash coming out but not where it's going). The more complex your estate is, the more one party (or both) is going to tire of trying to figure things out! The only winners in those cases are the attorneys (cha-ching, cha-ching).

Ultimately, you are the only one in the way of your financial happiness and peace of mind. If you sit in fear, then you will waste whatever time you have been given to grow and experience life with someone. Attitude is everything, and it will be contagious, regardless of whether you like the outcome. Show up and be positive, fearless, and courageous in your conversations. If the talks are difficult or if you receive pushback on the topics that mean the most to you (or you don't understand the topics that mean the most to your spouse), hit pause. But beware (insert flashing warning lights here): whatever is left unspoken during these conversations won't get any easier to address in the future. Rarely does love or time change a person's perspective on the matters that are core to their values. It may seem possible, but it comes with serious therapy, time, and commitment. It's critical to recognize financial differences up front and decide whether you can align or evolve together. Again, know your finances and your financial values. And have the hard conversations required to truly know those of your partner.

The Tough Questions

1. What are your financial goals? What happens if those goals are only yours to meet?

2. How important is money to you? What are you willing to pay or receive for peace? What conversations are you willing to have?

3. Do you have full knowledge of all your accounts, including credit cards? When is the last time you checked your credit rating and/ or the lines of credit available to you? How about those of your spouse? Even if your answer is "Yes, I am aware, as I handle all of our finances," look again! It can't hurt.

4. If you're thinking *I don't have time*, that means you don't want to *make time*. We all have the same number of hours in a day. Is there some-thing you are avoiding? What are you willing to modify in your routine to make time for the financial decisions and actions that matter?

5. Do you have an outstanding credit line or equity line on your home? If so, do you both have access to it?

6. Are you able to freeze accounts or withdraw funds?

Technically Speaking

Financial change may be in your future, so you need to understand how to make it work for you when and if such change happens. Here are a few steps you can take to empower yourself, heighten your awareness and know-how, and more confidently approach those hard conversations:

- Read, listen to podcasts, or follow reputable financial advisors online. Consider experts such as Jean Chatzky *(Money Rules)*, Dave Ramsey *(The Total Money Makeover)*, Napoleon Hill *(Think and Grow Rich)*, David Bach *(Smart Couples Finish Rich)*, and Robert Kiyosaki *(Rich Dad Poor Dad)*. They are a few of my favorites.

- I also highly recommend the Gottman Institute (https://www.gottman.com) and their research-based approach to making marriage work. If you're ready to have those real conversations with your partner *now* (and not when things get tough), take a read through *Eight Dates: Essential Conversations for a Lifetime of Love*.

5

Have Empowering Arguments Starting Now

THERE WERE THINGS in my childhood that felt normal until I was old enough to understand that they weren't. When my mom and dad met they were both divorced, each with two sons. I was the only child they had together and the only girl. Strangely, I never saw myself as having a blended or nontraditional family, nor did I see our situation as different or unique. Our daily lives revolved around career, school, and community. Our weekends were spent together as a family. My parents worked in the same office. My dad was a dentist, and my mother was his office manager (his assistant with benefits, if you will). Most of my youth was spent as the only child at home, with one babysitter from 9 a.m. until 3 p.m. and another from 3 p.m. until 9 p.m. When my parents were there, I would hear the ripple effects of a relationship that was lustful but also volatile and fraught with violence. At the points when the dysfunction would reach its heights, usually late at night, I would jump up and down on the floor above them hoping they would hear me and stop yelling. My parents loved each other in ways I only dreamed of experiencing as an adult and hated each other in ways I hadn't known were possible.

One of the nights most clearly etched in my memory occurred when I was eight years old. I spent it with my babysitter, Joberta, looking out the big picture window of our home. Jo-B's arms were wrapped tightly around me as I stood horrified, watching my father feverishly drive our family van around the circular driveway in front of our house with my mother hanging on to the driver's side window, clinging for her life. While I listened to them yelling at each other, my dad drove closer to the house, dragging my mother's backside through the prickly bushes. She was apologizing— begging forgiveness—and he was cussing like a sailor. I wondered what was so bad that she was making herself go along for that ride. Had she had an affair? Was she apologizing to prove her love? And what did my dad think he was doing by hurting her like that?

When my mother's cries for help were finally heeded, it was for nothing more than a bleeding fingernail. She got a Band-Aid . . . and Dad bought a gun. One night not too long after, he pointed that gun at my mother and me, threatening to rip somebody's tongue out. I can still hear his words and see the look on his face. My parents' split ensued, and I became my mom's sidekick in a private investigation that included spying on Dad and his new girlfriend (who happened to match more stereotypes than a *Baywatch* babe). My mom, two of my four half brothers, and I moved all of six houses down the street. We stayed nearby because my mother was convinced that they would eventually resume their (awful) marriage.

Every day we would drive by the house where my brothers and I grew up. I would see the basketball hoop I aimed for, the cactus I once accidentally sat on, the corner of the paved driveway where I would use chalk to draw imaginary train tracks, and the spot where I poured sugar so the ants could have a sweet meal. It felt as if I were living my life in slo-mo when our car crawled past the big picture window for those few seconds and we gazed into it, searching for my dad and his new girlfriend.

DIVORCE AND VOLATILITY FELT LIKE THE "NORMAL" I WAS MISSING IN MY LIFE.

Mom was an absolute disaster. Her divorce diet could have killed her if the cigarette smoke that billowed from her bedroom didn't take her first. I missed my parents being together, but ultimately, I wasn't sorry about the split because at least the violence had stopped. The pain, on the other hand, had just shifted. My mother began to experience the roller-coaster ride of grief and freedom that separation so often brings. Their decision to split was life-changing for me too. It was a path to better—but lonelier—days.

By the time I was given the option to leave for college at sixteen, divorce and volatility felt like the "normal" I was missing in my life. Loneliness had created opportunities for me that eliminated the need to prove my ability to outdrink, outsmoke, or outdo any college friend I was going to make. I kept to my own business and maintained a steadfast determination to never accept failure. I was on a mission to show everyone all the things I could accomplish. I also promised myself that I would never hang on to any metaphorical van, begging forgiveness for something I hadn't done or apologizing for hurt I hadn't known I'd caused. Boy, was I wrong.

The Flip Side of an Apology

When my marriage ended and I knew there was no going back, I sent Mr. Former a note that said nothing more than "I'm sorry." I wanted forgiveness for something that I finally felt was my fault. Dr. Harriet Lerner would be so disappointed. Dr. Lerner—a veteran clinical psychologist and author of *Why Won't You Apologize?*—has partnered with many other experts to explore and address the subjects of anger, intimacy, and even apologies. While some of my apologies to my ex over our decade-plus marriage were true apologies, the majority of them served only to de-escalate the conflict. Dr. Lerner would probably categorize my request for forgiveness as self-serving and unacceptable. It was for me, not for Mr. Former.

Dr. John Gottman's research shows that 69 percent of problems in a relationship are unsolvable.

(While that "69" may seem like a welcome number in certain aspects of your relationship, this is definitely not one of them!) Because the unsolvable percentage is so high, the key to success lies in how we deal with the remaining 31 percent. The Gottman Institute's Dr. Marni Feuerman says that "Trying to solve unsolvable problems is counterproductive, and no couple will ever completely eliminate them. However, discussing them is constructive and provides a positive opportunity for understanding and growth."[4] I'd agree.

TRUE, NON-SELF-SERVING APOLOGIES ARE RARE, BUT THEY DO EXIST.

What is a true non-self-serving apology? When I speak with my colleagues about apology, compassion, and helping to move others forward, I tell them the story of a client we'll call Ms. Fighting So Hard. She was a single mother of two going through a tumultuous divorce and having the most difficult time of her life. Her ex-husband had a serious drug addiction, leaving her emotionally widowed well before their split. When her case was over, she called to tell me she was sorry. I scratched my head and asked her why. We had won, and the case was over. There was nothing to be sorry about! She had done great! She explained that she was sorry the only version of her I ever got to see was the one who constantly felt attacked by her ex while she was fighting for her kids. That version of herself was tired, angry, overworked, and underweight. She wished I had gotten to see who she really was. It is one of the few apologies I have appreciated and understood. The rest of them, not so much.

The word "sorry" has too often become what we utter when we don't know what else to say or where else to start, particularly in cases of divorce. Some people will say they are sorry in order to hear the other person's point of view or their version of the story. And the strange silence that comes in between is uncomfortably awkward if you don't acquiesce! There is no dignity in this apology, but it carries on regardless. Saying you are sorry should never obligate the other human involved to return an apology. That would be like driving down a one-way street expecting oncoming traffic. It's not what "sorry" is intended to be.

Personally, unless I was digging deep and had

genuine remorse, I tended to use the word "sorry" in the way I learned from my mother: as a means to reduce conflict. There is no doubt that her generation of baby boomer women are known to apologize for everything. It is often used in an attempt to spare a repeat performance of the conflict. I was, for a time, guilty as charged. With my mom, work, community, and wife hats on at all times, it was typical to be late coming home or tardy to a dinner reservation. The profuse apologies would swirl like a cyclone around me as I attempted to overlove my way back into M.F.'s good graces. Sadly, my behavior was often met with the request to stop saying "sorry" if I wasn't going to change!

"SORRY" CAN ALSO BE A RELIABLE CRUTCH FOR SENSITIVE PEOPLE.

Those of us who have stockpiles of compassion, empathy, and understanding will recognize this pattern of behavior in ourselves. The problem with this kind of apology is that it can actually compound a problem (that you might not have known even existed) and exacerbate a shame mentality within you or your partner. While you are pleading for mercy, the bear is being poked, and "sorry" can quickly become a sad sentiment that leaves you feeling dark, alone, and resentful. Like a toy parrot stuck on replay, excessive apologizing quickly becomes a repeated pattern of victimhood and humiliation.

Twenty-year vulnerability, courage, shame, and empathy researcher Brené Brown said that some of the biggest and toughest questions she gets relate to apologizing, especially how to ask for an apology and how best to respond to an apology. On an episode of her podcast *Unlocking Us* featuring Dr. Harriet Lerner, Brown said that the way through hurt depends on our ability to deliver and accept an apology; however, as Dr. Lerner points out, "When apologies . . . go south, it will compromise a relationship."[5] I suggest taking that one step further and permanently shifting *the state of sorry* for yourself. Before you lean on that landslide of sorries, be sure to define what you hope to gain and where you are willing to go to find resolution.

Tips That Lead Us Astray

There are hundreds of tips for a lasting marriage that have both impacted and amused me over the years.

Some I have implemented enthusiastically. Some I've endured through gritted teeth. And some, I must admit, I've completely ignored. These include, but are most definitely not limited to the following:

- It's not work. You will just know what to do.

- Always say you're sorry; it's not worth the fight.

- Happy wife, happy life. (A man never gets to ask for what he wants?)

- Hugging and kissing your partner before you leave for work will keep you connected.

- Time will heal all wounds.

- When things are heated, let the other person leave and cool down. Return at a specific time for tea to discuss what started the argument.

- Have rules or off-limits topics for what you can and can't say during a fight.

- Have a safe word. (Contrary to what *Fifty Shades of Grey* has taught us, you don't need to have a red room to have a safe word.)

- Or one of my all-time favorites: if you have sex once a week and cook dinner every night, you will have a long-lasting marriage. (For the record, I tried it, and sex every Tuesday at 10 p.m. totally cripples spontaneity.)

All in all, I write to you as a divorced divorce attorney. None of these tips worked.

ONLY IN DISCOMFORT WILL THERE BE GROWTH.

What's so interesting to me is that amid the countless tips, most of which I tried, no one talked to me about the most critical part of a marriage: communication. A lack of real communication is debilitating, and "sorry" seems to have become so much more of a transactional word than a meaningful one. What are we seeking from all our sorries anyway? What are we bargaining for? Empathy? Peace? Understanding? Relatability? It's time to find a new way to resolve the need for forgiveness and find comfort with the discomfort you're feeling. Sit with the feeling. Get uncomfortable. Only in that discomfort will there be growth.

When it comes to a divorce case, I always tell my clients not to apologize. Saying you're sorry in our society often means you're assuming blame, and you don't need another mark in the "things you did or didn't do" box. Also, depending on how an attorney is handling a case, the focus is often on delivering the facts, and there's no time to be sorry! If you're busily apologizing, you'll be distracted from fiercely fighting for what you want or what you need. Saying you're sorry will not help move you forward, nor will it help with closure.

In the same way that we needed to shift from saying "I'm sorry" to saying "I'm here" when we learn someone in our life is newly separated, divorced, or reeling from loss of any kind, it's time to find an empowering alternative to all the sorries we say when we seek forgiveness or affirmation in our relationships (which, for some people, is constantly). Something that allows us to finish the sentence about the real cause and intention behind our sorries. As Lionel Richie suggests in his 1986 classic, it's time for more back-and-forth in our relationships, like "Say You, Say Me." Your arguments, conversations, and overall relationship should feel like a mutual exchange of energy, even in the highs and lows. After decades of hearing complaints about failed marriages, I have learned that if you want to save your marriage, you should try finishing the following sentence:

Have Empowering Arguments Starting Now

Starting now, I will . . .
Possible endings to this sentence include:

- actively listen.

- put more focus on understanding your needs.

- no longer be late (or at least I will do my best not to be—and I will communicate sooner if I will be).

- love you in a way that you understand.

- work toward a mutual exchange of energy, trust, and faith.

- stop accepting beliefs about myself that I know are not true.

- not say "I'm sorry" unless I'm willing to identify the purpose for my apology.

The list of variations of "starting now" sentences could be much longer. One thing is clear, though: marriage will be the hardest thing you will do (aside from becoming a parent, should you so choose). Finding compromise and putting someone else's interests ahead of yours on a regular basis is not necessarily easy or natural behavior. None of us wants to spend our days swimming in a sea of sorries and feeling like our needs are never met or our voices are never heard. "Sorry" is meaningless unless you know why you are apologizing. Do all you can to avoid reinforcing victimhood and getting caught up in the rinse-and-repeat cycle of assuming blame for everything. I highly recommend shaping a new pattern starting now because conflict is inevitable, and you'll want to be prepared for it as best you can.

The Tough Questions

If you're constantly apologizing, the most powerful question you can ask is, Have you forgiven *yourself*? Do you need to? (While exploring my need to constantly say I was sorry, my therapist prompted me to answer this question for myself. Until then, I didn't know that I hadn't forgiven myself.)

1. Are you truly sorry? I mean "regrettably sorry" and willing to not ever do it again?

2. Or are you saying you are sorry just to de-escalate the situation?

3. How is your partner contributing to the circumstances that make you feel apologetic?

Technically Speaking

Consider using a journal or joint email to communicate your concerns. This allows you and your spouse to see each other's perspective more clearly.

- Ask questions! Listen to hear, not to respond (or to be right).

- Share a hobby together such as bike riding, gaming, or playing music.

- Enjoy icebreakers or share books. Both can be fun ways to reengage you in the simple things that tie you together.

- Open yourselves up to couple's counseling and individual counseling (though the latter should not be done with the same counselor).

- There are excellent programs available all over the world for those who want to work on themselves and their marriage. Check out The Gottman Institute, Dr. Henry Cloud, or Marriage Quest, to name a few.

6

There Are No Winners When You Have a Swinger Over for Dinner

Mr. "I Did Not!"

THERE IS NO LAW that says you have to take a course on marriage (or divorce) before you enter into a partnership. When we marry, it's an agreement; when we divorce, it's the law. There are some laws that are worth taking into consideration, such as the alienation of affection law, though few even know of it because it's only applicable in six States. This law allows residents of those States to sue a spouse's lover for ruining their marriage. And I've seen it in action.

Several years back, I was co-counsel at a jury trial in a small town. Among other things, we had to prove that our client's wife had been sleeping with another man. With the boyfriend on the witness stand, the line of questioning began. "Isn't it true, Mr. I Did Not (as we will call him here to protect his identity), that you kissed my client's wife?"

He sternly replied, "Upon the advice of counsel, I plead the Fifth Amendment and refuse to answer the question."[6]

"Isn't it true, Mr. I Did Not, that you held hands with my client's wife?"

"Upon the advice of counsel, I plead the Fifth Amendment and refuse to answer the question."

"Isn't it true that you performed *cunnilingus with* my client's wife?"

Once again, he echoed, "Upon the advice of counsel, I plead the Fifth Amendment and refuse to answer the question."

His set-on-replay responses were getting old, but we pushed forward nevertheless, determined to see him break. "Isn't it true that you had vaginal intercourse *with* my client's wife?"

"Upon the advice of counsel, I plead the Fifth Amendment and refuse to answer the question."

"Isn't it true, sir, that you had anal intercourse *with* my client's wife?"

"I did not!" (Insert strong Southern drawl here.)

Mr. I Did Not was also married, and his family was sitting in the courtroom. There were no winners that day, though my client did prevail in the case.

WHAT YOU MIGHT NOT FIND ACCEPTABLE IN YOUR MARRIAGE, THE LAW MAY NOT CARE MUCH ABOUT IN DIVORCE.

There are always going to be cultural or community practices that are acceptable to some, such as having a boyfriend or girlfriend on the side, living by the philosophy of "what happens in Vegas stays in Vegas," or abiding by the 100-mile rule. Some may even embrace religions that preach "open love," though most times these practices are not accepted inside of marriage. Be forewarned, however, that behaviors you find unacceptable in your marriage may not be what the law cares about in divorce proceedings.

Did you know that States may differ in legal definitions including the definition of adultery? For instance, some do not require proof that there was actually sexual intercourse. Cases in certain States have held that the words "I love you" sent in text messages, or inappropriate pictures, small gifts, and even telephone conversations at odd hours are circumstantial enough to support cheating claims. Sometimes all it takes is establishing that the "opportunity and circumstances" were available so that if a spouse wanted and desired to have sexual intercourse or participate in illicit sexual conduct with someone else, they could have.

The impact of adultery may also differ depending on your State. For example, in South Carolina, adultery is believed to be the leading cause of fault-based divorce. It also applies until the day you are legally divorced. By contrast, North Carolina law states that marital misconduct ("sexual or deviant behavior") no longer applies *after* separation. Legally speaking, you can sleep with every player on the closest NFL team or the cheerleaders on the sidelines (or both, if you so desire), as long as you are separated in North Carolina.

In certain States, committing adultery may do nothing more than prevent you from receiving alimony. It will *not* fuel grounds for divorce and often will be used during trial only to highlight that the other person was not a faithful partner during your marriage (which is an emotional argument but not a legal one). And if you indicate to your spouse that they are forgiven for committing adultery, you may not be able to use cheating as a basis or grounds in your legal proceedings. I suggest that you tread thoughtfully, as the word "forgiveness" may be synonymous with the term "condonation." Check your State laws to understand whether you accidentally forgave your cheater or whether you were forgiven (and whether either even matters)!

The Cost of Sharing the Love

In the tantalizing 1999 movie *Eyes Wide Shut* starring Nicole Kidman and Tom Cruise, Cruise's character, Dr. Bill Harford, is shocked to learn that his wife, Alice (Kidman's character), considered having an affair. The awakening leads him to visit a secret society hosting wild orgies. Anyone who has watched the film likely has one particular scene permanently etched in their memory. My eyes were wide open when I saw all the beautiful naked people in masks. If you have an adventurous bone in your body, all parts of you wanted to replicate that scene in your own life. You know who you are.

Many a time, I have had consultations with clients who participated in a threesome or agreed to an open marriage for some period of time. And more often than not, they did so because something was missing in their marriage. The divorce lawyer in me can also attest that this kind of sexual exploration requires some serious stability, commitment, and communication. While such an arrangement may be okay for some, it is not for most—even couples with the strongest stability, commitment, and communication.

Not to get too 1990's Salt-N-Pepa on you, but let's talk about sex. You may have an overly adventurous sex life, or you may be living in separate bedrooms and wondering if you'll ever have sex with your spouse again. From a client's perspective, and as someone who has also experienced divorce, sex is one way we receive and give love. In almost every divorce consult, it is a central part of the conversation and one with substantial emotional meaning. Clients often realize after the fact how important intimacy was during their marriage and how it may have played into their divorce. Sex is very often the reason people *think* they are separating, but they are shocked when, in a divorce case where cheating is involved, the details of the conquest are merely skimmed over and considered inconsequential in the bigger scheme. Adultery ultimately boils down to the financial consequences of the decision (not the sex itself). So if you decide to "go there" and swing the night(s) away, you had better be ready for the financial shitstorm that is coming! And if you weren't the person involved in the adultery, the result is really going to piss you off. Lose-lose, people.

A ONE-TIME SWING IS NEVER A ONE-TIME THING.

A general social survey spanning from 2000 to 2016 revealed that, in general, men are more likely than women to cheat. In the survey, 20 percent of men and 13 percent of women reported that they've had sex with someone other than their spouse while married, and men tend to cheat more as they grow older, while the percentage of women cheating drops significantly.[7] If you think your partner is having an affair, they probably are. You need to follow your gut because a one-time swing is never a one-time thing, and an emotional affair is hardly ever just an emotional affair.

Side note: have you ever heard of a mister? Women beware. There's always a mistress but never a mister, so know the ramifications of your actions. A mister can slip away in the night, but a mistress will likely be shamed for the rest of her life. Can we either use both terms or abolish the term "mistress"?

When Things Get Hard (or They Don't)

One of the most trusted voices on relationships, Dr. Alexandra H. Solomon, suggests that where there is concern of cheating (or the impact of a sexually adventurous marriage), your best asset can be relational awareness—"the ongoing practice of understanding who you are in the context of your intimate partnerships."[8] Whether you are in the sexually adventurous camp or live in the house of intolerance, it's important to acknowledge your opinion and that of your partner with regard to sex and extramarital affairs, without judgement. Have the hard intimacy conversations up front. Does your partner have different expectations of you after the wedding day? Discuss it. If you choose to leave things to chance, you better keep your eyeglass prescription up to date and be on the lookout for the signs of adultery.

Cheating can all too easily become the straw that breaks your back, the source of relentless conflict, or the catalyst for a new baby in an extended relationship you didn't ask for. Even if US divorce rates have steadily decreased since the turn of the century,[9] there will always be factors such as the multibillion-dollar porn industry fueling the fire.

IGNORANCE IS NEVER BLISS AND BLISS IS ONLY ONE CLICK AWAY.

My advice: go into and through your marriage wide-eyed, but not wide open (to swingers, threesomes, communities, orgies, or the like). Don't have a threesome or bring a girlfriend or boyfriend into the mix and expect your marriage to thrive or survive. There are other ways to introduce excitement into the bedroom (or your life) than bringing in another human. There are no winners when one of you or both of you have a swinger for dinner. And for the record, trying to kill your spouse or even joking about killing your spouse for doing so will most likely end your marriage. Interestingly, it may not terminate your rights to be a parent.

The Tough Questions

If you knew the real consequences of marital misconduct, would you be more or less inclined to have an affair?

1. Do you have access to Internet history on all the devices in your home? Or are they cleared after each use? If they are, why is that so?

2. Do you feel like you or your partner is dissatisfied when it comes to intimacy? If so, what is your plan of action (since time alone will not be healing that wound)?

Technically Speaking

If you find out that your partner has committed or is possibly committing adultery, proceed with caution when deciding how to handle the situation. Here are some actions you can take:

- Look for a credit card account that you don't have access to, a code on a mobile device that you don't know, or an email account that you were unaware existed. (Beware if you can't access your partner's phone or don't have their passwords.)

- Look at your partner's apps. Did you know you can change the face of apps? What looks like the calculator might not be!

- Keep an eye on their phone for people's names saved under different numbers or numbers with changed names (e.g., naming a female friend "Jack").

- Beware burner phones as they are extremely difficult to track.

- Browse through the content on the iCloud for your family of devices. It can be telling, as can the invoices for mobile phones.

- Consult with an experienced family law attorney about your best course of action.

- In addition to saving bank statements, credit card statements, receipts, and other such records with activity that is "not normal," you may need to hire a private investigator to obtain evidence.

- If you are considering swinging, your actions can change your legal course, so proceed with caution and educate yourself before you stray.

- If you are tempted to have an extramarital affair, consider separating or divorcing first. If it's worth it, your mister or mistress will gladly wait. Find a new dopamine high (also known as the "happy hormone") quickly.

PART TWO

SEPARATION

NO ONE WILL KNOW HOW to tell your spouse that you are leaving better than you, and if you've resolved to break up, there's never going to be a good or easy way to do it. Alternatively, at any time and for any reason, your spouse could come home and tell you they don't want to "do forever" with you anymore. Read that sentence again slowly. Do you have a plan? Where will you go? How will you divide things? Who will stay in the house? Where will the kids go and when?

Technically speaking, the term "separation" is when you and your spouse no longer live under the same roof and one of you has the intention of no longer being married. Depending on your State, legal separation may or may not involve you and your spouse having a contract or court order. The obvious consequence of separation is that at some point (ranging from as little as sixty days in some States to as long as several years in others), you can legally divorce.

For some, separation provides the period of healing necessary to rekindle a marriage and find a way to make things work. For others, it represents the beginning of the end of a marriage. But before you even consider what life will look like on the other side, you need to ask yourself if you are prepared financially, emotionally, and logistically.

Separation is its own beast and its ultimate result in legal divorce will serve only as a punctuation mark on what is, for most people, a wildly challenging experience (because of the whole "the person you marry is not the person you divorce" thing). However painful, separation is also a temporary period leading to a more permanent period. It is not the beginning of the end, as so many people perceive it to be, but rather the start of something new—a new life *you* get to shape for yourself.

7

We All Use the Tissue Box

──────────○○──────────

Mr. Wall Street Shoes

WHEN NEW CLIENTS come into the firm for their initial consultation, I meet them in the big conference room. We sit at a giant solid wood table with six leather chairs on each side. Squarely in the middle of this massive table lies a box of tissues. I always let clients select their seat and curiously watch to see how many choose the chair at the end covered in animal-print fur. For some, their choice of seating represents a moment of empowerment during a time when things feel as if they are falling apart. For others, my strategy has absolutely no game.

One of my clients was a Wall Street type who made big money early in life. At six feet six, he strutted in wearing a sport coat, scarf, perfect glasses with perfect hair, and obviously expensive shoes. His skin was sun-kissed as if his life entailed an endless series of vacations. He was super smart and had that aura of health, well-being, and success. Every time he came in to see us, he would pick a new seat at the conference room table. "This seat looks like it was never used," he would say. It was obvious that his plan was to control the narrative and our meeting, but I was on to him.

Once we sat down and got to talking about his marriage, Mr. Wall Street Shoes broke down and cried. It was so interesting to watch someone who came in wearing so much emotional armor, ready to fight a war, fall apart and become so deeply human. His tears were not only for the loss of his marriage but also fear of the unknown. Even though he had been awful to his wife during the separation period, he sat before me accountable for his part of the equation, which I appreciated.

When most men come into the room for their first meeting, they are stoic in their approach, well-prepared, and seemingly put together. However, there are always exceptions, like the successful business owner who walked into the conference room, rested his forehead on the table, and just crumbled emotionally.

He did not want his marriage to end, and he hadn't yet told anyone what had happened. Stereotypically speaking, when women meet with me, they are usually more approachable and often teary-eyed. I've also had female clients who are some of the toughest, bravest women I've ever met, never once shedding a tear throughout the process. Their trick? They wait for the day they feel most courageous, pissed off, and finally done with feeling bad, afraid, and apologetic. Then they let it all out.

THE GRIEF ON THE OTHER SIDE OF SEPARATION DOES NOT DISCRIMINATE BASED ON GENDER, AGE, RACE, OR THE COLOR OF YOUR SKIN.

Like choosing a chair at the conference room table, everyone handles separation differently. Eventually, however, they all show their human sides. Regardless of whether you are an acclaimed athlete, a corporate executive, a respected school-teacher, or a busy homemaker, it's okay to fall apart. The grief on the other side of separation grips us all at some point. The tissue box sits in the *middle* of our conference room table because it doesn't matter which seat you choose; everyone is going to need it. And remember, regardless of which chair (or route to separation) you take, plenty of people have been there before you. In separation, you're likely experiencing something that you've never experienced before and for which you are not adequately prepared. The commonality among all who have been through separation and divorce is *change*. As you go through it, it's more than okay to cry and have compassion for yourself.

Relief and Disbelief

"You are the biggest mistake of my life." That was one of many, many not-so-lovely love letters I received from Mr. Former after ending our marriage. The "Mover of Funds" sent it after he finally transferred $100,000 back into our bank account. He had previously withdrawn that money without my knowledge (along

with cash equity in our home where I was living with the boys). One paid-off debt deserves another, right? I sure didn't think so, but he was clearly making a point about what he thought my emotional debt to him was.

Before we separated, I was under the impression that when you have a mature love, your partner only wants you to be happy. But after we separated, M.F. told me that I'd get what I deserved (and he'd get "justice" . . . whatever that meant). In his mind, justice had not been served for what I had "done to" him and our kids. And he shared his disdain regularly, direct to my inbox, in what I termed "The Weekly Beatdown." I truly wished he would put his "just" on "ice" and give his steadfast mission to "balance the scales" a rest. The clincher was a notice I received (clearly not intended for me) stating that his thirty-day Tinder account was about to expire. Were those the "plans" he was making just weeks after our split? I felt angry, sad, naïve, and numb. I also felt shame. I didn't know what direction to go in. I was experiencing this odd mix of relief and disbelief. Who was this human I thought I knew? I am sure he was thinking the same thing about me.

IT'S AMAZING HOW TWO PEOPLE CAN LIVE THE SAME EXPERIENCE SO DIFFERENTLY, SILENCED AND UNHAPPY.

I was trying to relate to this person with whom I had spent more than a decade of my life while listening to others tell me that he was a bad guy. Despite all the horrible and hurtful things he said to me, there were times when I missed him so much I couldn't stand it. The problem was that I really wasn't sure what I missed. The companionship? Knowing he was there? Knowing what to expect? Or was it knowing that he missed me (in some nondescript way that lay hidden deep between the lines of his barbed emails)?

I had written myself letters detailing what I would miss most about our marriage, and I even made a list of nonnegotiables to give him (with the hopes it would save us). Yet despite writing so much, I still didn't trust my feelings. In my not-so-quiet brain, I distorted whatever I heard from him. I didn't have apathy (as I probably should have had); I had empathy and compassion. Separation felt so big, so daunting. And in those times when it felt as if Mr. Former was desperate to have me back, I felt desperate to get my head on straight. All of this "feeling" stuff took me further and further away from the "doing" stuff that needed to get done.

I wasn't ready to get married when we did. Was separation my way out? Would I regret it? No. I couldn't pretend that the awful times in our marriage and hurtful words didn't happen. There are so many things you intentionally ignore when going through separation. And guilt, unfortunately, is *not* one of them. It is a big part of every internal conversation. Those damn *voices, voices, voices* in your head won't keep quiet.

When you said, "I do," however long ago that was, you committed to taking care of your spouse. Now you are struck by the reality that just because you're backing out (or your spouse is backing out) and one of you (or both of you) has become a totally different human, it doesn't mean that the relationship stops. Like it or not, you have to go through separation together.

For the record, writing helps, drinking does

not. Adrenaline-based activities also help, overeating does not (unless you're proactively preparing for the "divorce diet," which we'll talk more about later). In the midst of a separation, there is never going to be a blanket legal solution or one-size-fits-all approach, no matter how often your attorney pats you on the shoulder and says, "Don't worry about it."

WHEN IT COMES TO THE SEPARATION PROCESS, THERE IS NO SUCH THING AS "NORMAL."

"Normal" connotes "typical" or "expected," and there is nothing about the separation process that is any of those things. For this reason, not even the most qualified attorney in the world can tell you exactly what the best course of action will be or what decisions to make for your family and your circumstances. It's *your* family. The best thing you can do for yourself is form a network of people who are going to help you through the parts that your attorney is blind to. In most cities, there are local women's groups, men's groups, and faith-based groups that come together regularly to provide mutual support. Some groups of men or women start text threads or Facebook groups to support one another. Instagram posts from therapists are wildly helpful (and comfortingly private). What matters is finding people who have "been there" and can understand the emotional impact of divorce. I keep hearing one of my favorite authors, Glennon Doyle, echo in my ears: don't ask someone for directions to a place they've never been.[10]

The Obvious Consequence of Separation

The obvious consequence of separation is that, at some point, you will be eligible to get divorced. If you need the fastest divorce possible, you'd better hope you live in Alaska, where there is no durational requirement in a no-fault divorce, or in Kentucky, where the separation period is only sixty days.[11] In other States, such as North Carolina, where several of our offices are located, the separation period is a full year.

When some clients hear about the required waiting period, they say, "We can't get divorced for a year? Okay, I'll see you then." No! That is not what is intended by the extended timeline. Your separation period is not to be wasted—thrown away while waiting for better days. Nor should you be alone "in the wait." There is a reason why States such as Alabama, Louisiana (if you have children), New York, North Carolina, Maryland, Nevada, Ohio, Pennsylvania, Virginia, South Carolina, and Utah require spouses to hold off for a year between separation and divorce. During that period (when you can't legally become "unmarried"), you have an opportunity to work out your crap and make sure your decision to separate is the right one.

If you talk things out or think things through for long enough, you'll likely come to a decision that you either want to get back together with your spouse or that you absolutely need to end things. There usually isn't a lot of middle ground. Before you dive in and decide on the who, what, where, and when of life on the other side of separation, you need to make a final decision whether to stay married. For some, the separation process is a rude awakening that life on the other side of marriage will likely be much more strenuous from a financial perspective. Given that realization they decide to step back into their marriage. You may not personally want to start over (or have to work again if you hadn't previously had to work when married). Or you may not be ready to commit yourself to the process of healing and investigating what got you to the point of separation in the first place, though I hope you are.

If you have a shit ton to work through, here's hoping you live in Idaho where the period of separation is sixty months! In twenty States, how long your separation lasts will be up to you, your spouse, and the Courts, as there is no identified period of separation before you can divorce. Use that time wisely. Start by consulting a divorce lawyer. If they are anything like me, they will be *very* real with you about what to anticipate and may even scare you back into your marriage. Separation and divorce are never going to go down the way you expect. Some things are going to be out of your control and are going to hurt, but once you've run out of tissues and you've pulled yourself up off the ground, you ultimately get to make your own choices.

The Tough Questions

1. Is separation truly the right choice for you?

2. What will your partner say is the reason you are getting divorced?

3. Are you allowing the voices of fear inside your head to direct your fate?

4. What are you stopping yourself from doing or saying to your spouse?

5. What are you accepting about yourself that you know is not true?

6. How have you evolved since you said "I do"? What about your spouse?

7. What expectations do you have of each other? How willing are you to manage those expectations throughout the separation process?

Technically Speaking

- Find a group of humans who can truly understand what you are going through. (Preferably, they're the kind whose armor is not so thick that they don't cry.)

- Know what your coping mechanisms are and what works for you. (And have faith in and compassion for yourself.)

- Start to think about what life looks like with/for your children on the other side of separation. (Preferably, you'll do this *before* you separate.)

- Go see a divorce attorney. People who do what I do professionally care about how things are going to be divided, what financial support is going to exist, and where your kids will rest their heads every night.

- If you have chosen separation or divorce, do the necessary research to determine which attorney is the right one to help you take your next steps. Because those steps are going to happen whether you like it or not! The American Academy of Matrimonial Lawyers and board certifications in the area of family law are worthy of consideration, but they may not be the voice you want or need.

- National and local bar associations have separate sections specifically for family law attorneys. However, not all family law attorneys are created equal, nor do they have the same philosophies on resolution, so choose wisely.

- Consider an attorney's involvement in the community (legal and otherwise), their published written work, and the comments they have written in social media to ensure you like their general opinions and that they are evolving and capable of thinking outside the box. It will be your life they are changing. Your family deserves better than a one-size-fits-all solution.

- Create a journal to track your thoughts, questions for your lawyer, and comments from your spouse that you think your lawyer will want to know about. Also start a parenting calendar to help organize yourself and draft a list of expenses that will ultimately end up looking like a budget.

8

It Doesn't Have to Be the Worst Thing That's Ever Happened

ONE COLD SATURDAY morning, my sidekick (aka my dog, Gigi) and I flew across town in just enough time to make my youngest son's soccer game. It was my week without the boys, but I couldn't remember ever missing a game, even when they weren't with me. I always wanted them to see that Mr. Former and I have the shared purpose of making them feel cared for, happy, and loved. Not to mention, I am also an avid sideline mom. I showed up in my soccer team ball cap and had a second team ball cap with me for my middle son's football game later that day (because I wasn't already wearing enough hats as a divorced, business-owning mother of three with a dog by my side). From a clothing perspective, I was fully prepared; from an emotional one, I was not.

I walked onto the field like a proud sideline mom with my chair, enough drinks for the boys (in case all three of them were there), and a blanket in tow. Oh, and two extra chairs in the car in case anyone wanted to sit with me. Knight in shining armor? Romeo, oh, Romeo? Anyone? Nope, no takers. Well then, to keep myself from freezing in forty-degree weather, I propped Gigi on my lap and nestled close against her fur. When the game ended, I made the necessary switch into the team-appropriate hat and then drove to the other side of town to watch the football game. The boys traveled with my ex, his girlfriend, her siblings, and her parents (their other family). When we arrived at the field, they all sat together on one side. I sat alone at the end of the field.

The game, as always, was intense, like a real-life version of the television drama *All American*. There was camaraderie, community, and some good old-fashioned competition. When it came time to leave, something happened for which I was wholly unprepared. As the crowd walked away from the field, I was surrounded on all sides by families but none of them was my own. I was ten yards behind and ten yards to the right of my boys and their "other family." Talk about being the odd mom out! I can't recall ever feeling more obviously and sadly alone. Two of my boys slowed so that I could hear them repeating, "Bye, Mom, I love you. Bye, Mom, I love you." Then as we all reached the top of the hill, they went one way, and I went another. I got in the car and cried. My heart and soul were left scattered somewhere around the ten-yard line.

Before you're separated or divorced, no one ever tells you what it will feel like to leave without your children. Why did it hurt so much to have to leave alone? Was it because I was literally by myself? (No offense, Gigi.) Was it because my kids were heading off with another family? Was it sadness or envy? Was it punishment because it was my decision to not be in the marriage anymore? I wanted to be able to better manage the situations for myself. I wondered what it brought up for the kids and if they would adapt. Looking at them from ten yards behind, they seemed fine. But doesn't "fine" really just mean "f*ed up, irrational, neurotic, and emotional" when we are adults?

NO ONE WHO SAYS "FINE" EVER MEANS IT!

There was a lot of emotional digestion and examination to do that day. Why had that event triggered me, and what could I learn from it? I wrote myself a note because I didn't want to forget what it felt like to walk alone and to have to leave my boys. I flashed back to the day of my high school graduation, when I could see my mom and two of my brothers, off to the right of the crowd, but I couldn't see my dad. My parents insisted on not sitting together at events. I remember searching everywhere for my father. He told me he was there, and I believed him—until I didn't.

There is no easy way to prepare yourself for all the aspects of separation. People will happily share their (unhelpful) tips as you go through it. They will say things like, "Separation is the best time to get plastic surgery" or, "Have a divorce party and name a cocktail after yourself." While humorous, these silly notions will not ease the fact that separation, no matter what it looks like, is *not* going to be easy (though a divorce party and drinking to "adios m*ther f*cker" may temporarily relieve some pain). When a client tells me, "This is going to be really easy," I immediately shake my head in disagreement. Much like opening a can of worms, once you and your spouse separate, the beast is unleashed, and there's no putting it back no matter how hard you try. Remember, it takes *two* people to make an agreement (plus lawyers to advocate so their respective clients don't get screwed). The process can be difficult, volatile, and even unfair, but it doesn't have to be the worst thing that's ever happened to you. You just have to separate strategically and plan from the beginning.

Breaking Down What You Built

Depending on the State you live in, sometimes when you separate you will be immediately treated as though you are unmarried even though you are not yet legally divorced. Know your State laws and also know that sometimes it's really just a matter of semantics. *Marriage or no marriage, when you separate there is no longer an intact family as you knew it.*

Regardless of who initiated the process or where you reside, it can be very difficult to make decisions and plans in the midst of separation. As you journey, *you may not know what you want.* Making decisions can become scary, and you can start to question yourself.

YOU ALSO MAY NOT TRUST YOURSELF TO MAKE THE RIGHT DECISION (IF YOU EVEN THINK YOU KNOW WHAT THE RIGHT DECISION IS!).

As you navigate your new normal, you have to get used to a new schedule, and you may no longer have a partner in the other parent. When it comes to breaking down the aspects and assets of the life you built with your spouse, there will be some obvious, big questions that come up:

- How will we divide things?
- Where will the kids lay their heads every night?
- Do we file taxes together or independently?
- Who gets the house? Do I have to buy my spouse out?

There will also be more intricate questions:

- When should I tell my partner that I am going to move out?

- Should I move out, or should I wait for my spouse to do it?

- Do I take all my things?

- If I leave, can I come back? Will my spouse change the locks?

- If my name is still on the mortgage and title, doesn't that count for something?

- What if my spouse doesn't pay the mortgage?

- Do I have to pay alimony instead of putting our eldest through college the way we always promised? Who should come first?

- Should I pay off my credit card?

- My lease is up for renewal; can I still afford to live here?

And of course, every case inevitably has a car question:

- I need a new set of tires; can I get them? Or can I just get a new car?

Answering the hard questions always involves

a balance between listening attentively and pushing others and yourself into action. Separation is not for everyone, but if you decide that it is your best path, the ideal thing you can do is prepare yourself by planning what life post-separation will look like *before* either of you moves out. Because entering into separation or divorce does not automatically resolve how your property or things will be distributed. (I once had a mediator tell me that he wished separating couples would immediately sell their house because a family home can be a very difficult asset to support on a single income.)

WAITING TO MAKE THESE TOUGH DECISIONS MEANS YOU RISK SETTING PRECEDENT.

If you define each of your parental and partnership roles and responsibilities as "the person providing support" and "the person receiving support," there will be fewer unknowns. You won't be left with questions about who will pay the bills and where the kids will sleep. Waiting to make these tough decisions means you risk establishing an unacceptable plan, losing evidence, having to be without health insurance, or not knowing who your insurance beneficiaries are. If you have a joint account, be forewarned: either of you could empty it without the other's permission. (Remember my whole blonde-bombshell-at-the-bank moment?) Yes, yes you can. But should you? The best thing you can do from the beginning is know where your money is and how you are going to distribute it because, as you now know, when the money is gone, no lawyer—no matter how successful or powerful they are—can hand it back to you.

If you're the one leaving the house, do you know when you'll see your kids once you separate? Are you okay with not knowing? These are the issues that can drive someone back to being more committed to their marriage. Custody is a whole other ball game. Some of my most memorable legal experiences have been in custody cases. While emergency cases may be handled quickly, temporary or permanent decisions take much longer (years in some larger jurisdictions). And when it comes to children, nothing is ever really permanent. Your children age, needs change, schools change, and in certain instances the Court may be able to modify a "permanent" agreement. (What isn't mentioned here is domestic violence or withholding the children—other issues that come along with separation at times.)

Ultimately, the aim is always to get a full and clear view of the situation (like from fifty thousand feet up!) and see how the assets are to be distributed, the kids are to be taken care of, and support is to be paid (if it is deemed necessary). Separation is about understanding your new normal and finding the opportunity for positive and effective growth. And yes, this new normal means that you can open your own bank account. By the way, consider this a PSA for the nonworking parents out there: you may need to start establishing your own credit. This is very real and scary as hell for parents who haven't worked and need to refinance a house or apply for a credit card.

Reconciling the Unreconcilable

I once drafted a reconciliation agreement for a woman whose spouse had committed adultery. She was the supported spouse. In an environment where trust was hard to reestablish, the agreement detailed what would happen financially if they couldn't make their marriage work. The goal of the agreement was to remove financial leverage and create solutions that forced them to focus on their relationship. As a divorce attorney, I always want to set clients up for a new beginning, one they can craft with what they have in their arsenal. Before I tell my clients anything about the law and how things will play out, I always ask, "What do you want out of this?" Separation agreements (or reconciliation agreements) are useful contracts that identify what roles you are each going to play, which may also extend beyond the agreement and post-divorce. They can start off something like "In the event of an unfortunate separation, these are the rules that will be in place." Often referred to as a post-nuptial agreement (and much like a prenup), the agreement defines what things will look like in terms of the financial ramifications, asset distribution, and so on if you and your spouse separate.

Now the caveat: it takes two to "make these things go right" and to gain agreement on the terms. Both of you have to want to focus on the relationship. When I presented Mr. Former with a post-nuptial agreement, he said that if it wasn't about the money, I wouldn't have asked him to do a post-nup. Was our trust already broken? I felt so threatened. When I offered the document, it was with the intention of our being able to focus on our relationship, not some "hocus-pocus, make our money disappear" magic!

There are ultimatums (and often the revelation of someone's true colors) that come with a post-nuptial agreement, and they are very real. If you want to make separation difficult, it will be difficult. However, if you want to make it easy (or easier), it can be that instead. If you go in thinking separation and divorce are the worst things that have ever happened to you, then you will *make them* the worst things that ever happened to you! No, you can't magically flip a switch and change your ex's behavior, but having a good mindset and some extra knowledge will help get you through the experience (that whole "when you know more you can do more" idea).

THERE WILL NEVER BE AN EASY OR BEST TIME TO MAKE THE HARD DECISIONS AND TAKE THE TOUGH STEPS.

You can manage separation, but you must have the courage to move forward without questioning your every move. You may decide to clean out the house while your spouse is away on vacation. Or you and your spouse may decide together that separation is your best option. A civil conversation should help, but you won't be able to control the response of the other human, no matter how or when those dreaded words "I want to separate" are spoken.

The Tough Questions

1. Why would your partner say you have ended up sitting in a divorce attorney's office? (Tell the whole story. No sugarcoating. Your attorney can't protect you from surprises that pop up later.)

2. What would your partner say is the worst thing about being married to you? (Tough question, I know, but these are things that will come up in court.)

Technically Speaking

- When discussing how to resolve the issues of financial support, property distribution, and custody, listen more and talk less. That way, you won't have questions about who is paying the bills or how the property might eventually be distributed. You don't have to agree to everything up front, but at least use the time as a baseline for understanding the other party's perception or belief.

- Think about (and track) what you spend so you can create a personal budget. (This one is on the "homework list" I give clients.) If there is already a family budget, provide a copy to your attorney (include prior year budgets if they exist).

- Download apps to help with co-parenting or managing your finances. They can be useful guides.

- Create a separate email account where you can store everything related to your divorce. Gather everything you think you might need and everything your lawyer might need. When all is said and done, you can let the email account die with the relationship.

- Take a picture, screenshot, or screen record of any communication from your ex that you think could be worth sharing with the Court. Send them to yourself at the separate email account you created.

- Turn off your iCloud and change your passwords.

- If you are the one who stays in the house, you may decide to change the locks to create a physical boundary (as well as an emotional one). If you do this, don't forget about the garage door opener and the security system!

- If you are the one who moves from your home, know that the person who remains in the home may be able to change the locks and the only way back in is by agreement or court order.

- Make every attempt to create a separation agreement. If you're in a situation where your lawyer isn't helping you find a solution, you have two choices: find another lawyer or create the agreement yourselves and take it to a lawyer for proper drafting.

9

Your Children Can Hear You (and See You)

NO, CONDOMS aren't balloons. The eggplant emoji doesn't mean you are going to be forced to eat eggplant parmesan. Daddy isn't going to kidnap you just because he drives a different way home. Mom getting a new car doesn't mean she got a new job. Kids will make assumptions. They hear (and see) everything and repeat it often, even if what they repeat is far from accurate. In more serious times, they may echo what they have heard or have been told, and what they say can become the foundation of a client's case. Other times, they may also create their own stories seemingly out of nowhere.

In one of my cases, a teenage girl was mad at her

dad because, well, she was a teenager. It didn't help that her mom regularly convinced her that her dad wasn't a good guy. The weight of her woes, and the seesaw she felt she was on because of the separation, led her to lock herself in her room whenever she was at her dad's home. One night, she reported that he beat her. After going through months of litigation to rebuild his credibility and convince the Court that he would never lay a hand on his daughter, the judge ordered equal parenting time with both parents. His daughter finally admitted she'd made the story up because she was upset that he had taken away her phone and didn't allow her to go to a party. Even after this father fought for time with his child so he could repair their relationship, she refused to reunite with him.

Parents are often focused on telling *their* truth in these high-conflict situations. As a parent, it's easy to think that we know our children well, but we don't always consider such factors as emotional development and the consequences of our own choices on our children. When kids repeat what they have heard, rarely does a parent respond with, "It's my fault." There can be a failure to acknowledge how our children are receiving what they are hearing. It can also be common for parents to fear what their kids may report, even falsely. When it happens, parents definitely don't see it coming, and it can change their lives forever.

Parents also parent differently, regardless of whether they are together or separated. But during separation, kids are regularly forced to discern fact from fiction and what is silly from what is serious. They may struggle with loyalty and either parent may ask so much of them (without even knowing it), that the child may form perceptions (or misperceptions) and make up stories.

WHATEVER CHOICES YOU MAKE, YOU ARE GOING TO FEEL THEM AND YOUR KIDS ARE GOING TO FEEL THEM TOO.

When you are separated or divorced and living in two different homes, you have to become very conscious of what you say. Choice is one of the most powerful ways to implement change in your life. But recognize that whatever choices you make, you are going to feel them. Your kids are going to feel them. And your pets are going to feel them too. Your children can read, they can see, and they can hear. If you're going to change your ex's name to "Be-otch," "Arse," or "Do Not Answer" in your phone, be ready for that to backfire big-time, as your kids will no doubt start calling them by those names as well. A client I represented was once punished in a ruling because she listed her ex-husband as "Pennywise" on her phone and her child read it.

Kids will ask or echo just about anything:

- Mommy is going to the big house. (No, not prison.)

- Daddy now plays with a different team.

- What is "morning sex"? I saw it on your text messages. (You might want to consider reducing the font size on your screen.)

- What is Tinder? Does it sell soft toys?

I live in a State where the law dictates that we do what is in the best interests of the child. If you're expecting your children to self-report how they are feeling on a regular basis or you believe they may never lie to you, it's time for a reality check. They might lie. They might also embellish or create their own version of reality. Don't rely on your children for anything other than just to be your children.

Different Interpretation, Same Level of Pain

Although Mr. Former and I discussed telling the children that we were taking a "time-out" before our fighting became apparent, we didn't. Until the day we physically separated, it felt as if our fights followed the same cycle: he would yell, tell me again and again how he felt, and then he would leave the room (or wherever we were). These one-way shouting matches continued into our separation and so did their impact on our boys. One night, we were fighting upstairs. Because I had closed the door, M.F. yelled, "Let the children hear me!" Following the argument, two of our boys had very different interpretations. Our eldest son asked me, "Mommy, why are you so bad? Why is Daddy always yelling at you?" His younger brother said, "Daddy is such a bully, Mommy. I'm sorry you're so sad." Then he gave me a big hug.

There are parents who hope their kids will hear them. They somehow believe they know how the children will receive their words. In some ways, we all think our children can handle more than they can. I've also had clients who freely say things because they think their children *won't* understand. But that's not a safe assumption. Though they may not comprehend, your children sense the tension just the same.

EVEN IF YOUR KIDS CAN'T HEAR YOU, THEY LIKELY CAN STILL SEE YOU AND FEEL THE IMPACT OF YOUR WORDS.

Here's a scenario that happens all too often (and one where the audio was played in court). One day, a father called his son while the son was at the mother's house. Mom answered and yelled to her son, "Your dad is on the phone!" When the son picked up the phone, the dad decided to rant about his mother being a "F-ing bitch." He also said he wished she would die. The onus was now on the son to do something about this behavior. Of course, the dad thought his son was in his court (in both senses of the word). Things went terribly south for the dad when the mom, who was still on the line, recorded every nasty word her ex uttered about her and gave the recording to me to present to the Court. The dad's attempt to align with his son and alienate his ex-wife backfired, *big*-time. The son saw things differently than his dad. From the boy's perspective, the father was being a bully and the mother was the victim. I'm pretty sure the dad learned a lesson that day he won't ever forget.

Your children's perceptions of events may not be what you assume they'll be, and two children from the same household can also hear things very differently. The point is that all too often parents are willing to roll the dice and take a chance on how their children will interpret their words and actions (or they don't even consider the possible fallout before they speak or act). When I'm on the phone with a client, I'll typically ask if their kids can hear them. They all say no. Then, midway through our conversation, I inevitably hear a child in the background. Your children can hear you. And these are the kinds of circumstances that lead to the sobering statistics associated with kids of divorced parents! It doesn't have to be that way.

Don't Hide Behind Your Children

During my marriage, I cried when I needed to cry. I can't say the same was true for Mr. Former. After we separated, my boys only saw me cry twice, but M.F. cried often and our boys knew. He said that it was good for them to know how he felt. Early in our separation, our eldest son would physically place himself so he blocked his dad's view of me. He wanted to protect his father because he knew that M.F. would become visibly upset whenever he saw me. My ex told me that he didn't notice this happening (probably because our son was in the way)! When one parent doesn't see what is going on, the situation has the potential to go unaddressed, adding to the impact on your children.

Call it parental neglect or just plain self-serving: your children should never be the ones protecting you or gathering information for you (like a mother bringing her daughter along on her quests to spy on her ex in his new life). Your children should also not be the ones to have to communicate what is going on between you and your ex. They have no control or choice in your separation, so don't put them in a situation where they have to become the parent and you become the child.

Psychiatrist and family therapist Ivan Boszormenyi-Nagy and his coauthor, Geraldine M. Spark, are known for, among other things, giving a name to this phenomenon back in 1973. They called it "parentification" and identified it as "the process through which children are assigned the role of an adult, taking on both emotional and functional responsibilities that typically are performed by the parent. The parent, in turn, takes the dependent position of the child in the parent-child relationship."[12] I think it's good to let the children in on age-appropriate things, but you have to question whether your children have the emotional maturity to handle what you are throwing their way, especially when it is done regularly or in excess.

IT'S SO IMPORTANT TO UNDERSTAND HOW VULNERABLE (AND WISE) YOUR CHILDREN CAN BE.

Failing to understand the impact of the role reversal on children and their developmental perspective can cause real emotional damage. Unless you fully grasp what is developmentally appropriate for them (read: you are a trained psychologist or psychiatrist), at no time should you be making such a determination for them. Kids are socially and emotionally perceptive. It's hard for them not to want to protect or "fix" emotionally wounded parents. They can easily start to think, *I'm so worried about you, I need to protect you.* That's a launch point for parentification. For your child's sake, never put them in that position or role, because once they take it on, there is no telling how long they will stay there or how it will begin to affect their other relationships. Don't be that couple who doesn't care what the kids see or hear (unless, of course, you want your child to turn out to be one badass divorce attorney!).

Bill Eddy, cofounder of the High Conflict Institute and author of *Don't Alienate the Kids: Raising Resilient Children While Avoiding High-Conflict Divorce*, often references the 2010 parenting study published in *Scientific American Mind*.[13] The study of thousands of parents identified three top parenting skills: love and affection, the ability to manage your own stress, and healthy relationship skills with your coparent. Eddy talks about how these reactions shocked everyone because nowhere was there mention of managing your child's behavior.[14]

Children learn from your example, and they need at least one parent to be their rock, their foundation. Take all measures possible to protect your children and don't hide behind them! Unless you fully understand what is developmentally appropriate, don't do what can't be undone or say what can't be unsaid in front of them (and subsequently the Courts, especially if your ex pulls out a recording of your comments). Ultimately, you should always consider the impact of your separation on your children and do what you can to be proactive supporting them through it.

The Tough Questions

1. Do you know what is developmentally appropriate for each of your children to hear and what their coping mechanisms are when they're under stress?

2. How will you communicate with your kids when you aren't with them? Who provides and pays for their devices? Do both parents have access or is that unnecessary?

3. Who covers the travel cost if the children are traveling between homes? What about gas or car repairs for your teenage drivers? Sitter fees? New or lost PE uniforms? Broken retainers?

4. Who covers health insurance and what is the cost to you and the children if the plan changes? What is the deductible? Who is responsible for the uninsured expenses (copays, therapy, and so on)? How and when are you reimbursed? Where is the EOB (explanation of benefits) sent? Who has online access to these records?

5. What are your coping mechanisms when you find yourself under stress and triggered?

Technically Speaking

- Visit with your child's school guidance counselor, tell them what is going on, and ask them to check on your children. That's their job! But remember, what you tell them is not confidential.

- Your children need to see your support. Each parent is important to them.

- To help keep coordinated (and keep the peace), create a separate email account under your kid(s)'s names that *both* parents can access, for example, joeandjane@gmail.com. Add it to your phone and give that email address to all of your children's coaches, teachers, doctors, and so on. Use it so that there are no questions (or at least fewer questions) about communication, appointment times, practice or game times, or their grades.

10

Cheerio, Confidentiality!

―――――○○―――――

Pimp Parking at the Diner

WE TALKED ABOUT children hearing and seeing your every action, but in separation, you never know who else is listening or watching. I once heard a judge say to a client, "Now you know I'm watching. If that's what you did when you *didn't* know I was watching, I can't wait to see what you do when I am watching!"

When I was a young lawyer, my boss asked me to join in a consult with him on a new case. Sitting in that meeting, I heard the husband declare that his wife's relationship with her secret boyfriend was ruining their marriage. On a daily basis, our client's wife would get up, kiss their kids, and then meet her boyfriend at the local diner. After her "breakfast," she would return home, kiss their children goodbye, and wave as her husband took them to school.

Now, the wife's idea of having breakfast was backing into a parking space at the diner (which I fondly refer to as "pimp parking") with her boyfriend. What exactly happened in that car? Well, after the husband sent a private investigator to monitor the wife's morning routine, the investigator reported back that all he could see was her head bobbing up and down on her boyfriend's lap. Is that keto-friendly?

As you go through your separation and divorce proceedings, you are going to hear things about your ex (and maybe even yourself) you won't believe. A blow job you might believe, but leaving every single morning to meet your lover at the diner for some good old-fashioned head-bobbing before your kids go to school is a lot for any spouse to stomach.

Soon after that morning spy mission at the diner, I was out to dinner with friends (and some of their friends) when I did what I had done with every new lawyer who came into our firm: I told them this crazy story. I changed some of the facts and fudged the number of children, but I described this deliciously salacious tale from my new career. As I enthusiastically told them about this wife's thrilling escapades, the girl sitting to my right said, "God, my best friend just got busted for doing almost the same thing." As it turned out, she was the wife's best friend and knew the facts of the case. I calmy excused myself from the table, went to the bathroom, threw up, and called my mother.

In life, most of us are careful about what we disclose to others. When you go through separation and divorce, the rules are especially heightened. The only confidentiality that exists is between you and your lawyer. In our mobile-phone-using society where credit and debit cards are the currency of choice, your every move becomes trackable. When you use your credit card or coupon code at the grocery store, you never know how your purchases could be interpreted. Pull out your (trackable) reward points card and it may have consequences. What you text or email is no longer private, either, though it never really has been. When you are separated, someone is interested in watching your every move. And if you think you can take out your fears and frustrations online with friends, don't. Social media will burn your ass, especially when a lawyer decides to cross-reference your post with your friend's, your Snapchat location, your credit card, your IP address, and so forth. If you're a business owner, buckle up; divorce will be doubly daunting because both your personal and professional lives may be under scrutiny.

YOU WILL FEEL AS IF SOMEONE IS LOOKING OVER YOUR SHOULDER WITH EVERY TRANSACTION. EVERY TIME. EVERYWHERE.

Finding Trusted Allies

I know how difficult it is for most people to even pick up the phone and call a divorce attorney, much less come into my office and tell me the quiet, undisturbed memories of their marriage—the memories they wanted to forget, the ones they never thought they would have to tell a stranger. Nothing clients share with me gets repeated unless they want it to be repeated. I am a safer lockbox than their doctor, their therapist, and definitely their spouse. Unless a client tells me that they are going to kill themself or someone else, their secrets are safe with me and anyone under the employ of the firm.

However, it's not always up to me. The challenge is that when litigation ensues, the stories you wanted to keep undisturbed can become the testimony of the person you once called your partner for life. No lawyer representing your interests—no matter how loyal he or she is to you—can promise that what you tell your doctor or therapist won't be admissible at some point in time. If there is a custody case and your mental health is called into question, details might be considered relevant and become part of the case. In a high-conflict situation, the promise of confidentiality you may not have received or accepted is not always deemed relevant, no matter how private your disclosure. You need to make a choice early on as to whether you can manage the fallout. Because, just like an objection in the Courtroom, even if it's sustained, it can't be unheard!

When M.F. would fire at me during our fights like an emotional AK-47 with endless rounds of ammo, I had to learn how to ignore him because returning fire was not the best course of action and would only come back to me like a grenade latched onto a boomerang. If you've ever tried it, you can understand how difficult it is to bite your tongue under such an attack. I think Bill Eddy would have given me a 7.2 out of 10 for my effort.

In the never-ending struggle to discern what you can say or do without getting sucker punched by it in court, you might feel as though you've become a crazy person talking about a crazy person. You start to question what is relevant and what is not, what to say and what to avoid saying at all costs. You're not sure which one of the voices in your head to listen to at any moment. You're afraid to pull cash out of the ATM and afraid to make a deposit. As a client talking to an attorney, you don't know if you can trust having a good old-fashioned tell-all conversation or if you should cherry-pick your evidence and story. You have no idea what to expect from choosing either of these routes or the one that cuts straight down the middle. All these choices can leave you afraid to make a move of any kind. Just remember this: you can alter a story and change the facts, but when you do the dirty or tell a tale about it, even a big town can feel like a small town very quickly (and the four walls of a courtroom can close in on you just as fast).

IF YOU NEED TO CALL YOUR LAWYER TO ASK THEM IF SOMETHING YOU'RE THINKING OF DOING IS OKAY, IT PROBABLY ISN'T!

Resist the urge. You want to be credible, honest, and always act in the best interests of your children. When it comes to keeping your confidentiality (and sanity), the best you can do is keep your eye on the ball. Instead of dwelling on who may be watching you and when, focus on your integrity. Concentrate on today (and not the whole divorce marathon). Focus your attention on your kids and on being a good parent. These are things you can control.

The Tough Questions

1. Have you selected a therapist who is willing to navigate this tricky terrain with you? Will he or she destroy their notes after your sessions?

2. Is there any "nuclear option" material about your spouse that you may need to have in your back pocket (if things turn into an all-out war)? Or is there anything your spouse may have in their back pocket about you?

3. Do you have pictures on hand to use as evidence (photos of property damage, records of how much someone spends on alcohol each month, and so on)?

4. What are you willing to leverage?

Technically Speaking

- Before you hit the record button, find out if your State requires consent of both parties to record a conversation legally.

- Identify a safe word for your therapist or physician to stop taking notes when what you are sharing verges on testimony territory.

- Some journals come complete with a pack of matches (in case you need to blow things up in advance of them blowing up on you). Otherwise, ask your attorney for instruction on what is privileged or directed by him or her for court preparation.

11

Simplify and Let Yourself Screw Up

○○

A Literal Loss of Power

WHEN SEPARATING, it's hard not to stand in your kitchen and *remember a time when*: the kitchen was where you celebrated a new job, cried over a loss, or carved pumpkins (and Thanksgiving turkeys). A lot of people will look for things to change during and after separation. They seek distractions so they don't have to deal with the mounting feelings of emptiness and the loss of control. The first thing I did post-separation was renovate my kitchen.

A month later, the boys and I were standing in the newly remodeled room when a flyer came in the mail. A house in the neighborhood had just gone up for sale. It had a pool and more space than we would ever need. The boys were all about it! Frankly, since the three of them came into the separation without any choice, I wanted them to feel as if they had a choice in *something*, even if moving was most definitely not on my radar. It was noon when we read the flyer and 2 p.m. when we arrived at the house for a walk through with the listing agent. Two days later, we were under contract to buy the house. *Sold!*

I made the leap without any idea how I was going to pay for it. It happened too quickly for us to sell our other house first, and who knew how my divorce journey was going to shake out financially. What's more, I was still cleaning up some of the remains of our estate, running a multioffice law firm, taking care of clients and employees, and trying to start a new healthy relationship. It was such an overwhelming time, but the boys were on top of the world. They were so happy with their new handpicked home. Although I felt buried somewhere near the earth's crust, trying to find my way through to my new normal and a new life, I reminded myself that I was in charge, that I was determined, and that I was still a supermom. Nothing could get in my way, right? I made lists, and with some superhuman strength, I managed to check every box as we moved into our new home . . . or at least, I tried.

IT WAS GOING TO BE THE SCREWUP OF THE CENTURY!

Two months after settling into our new place, I was preparing dinner with the boys when *poof*—the gas on the stove went out. I immediately called the gas company and told them there had been a *giant* mistake and I needed my gas turned on as soon as possible. I started to cry. I told the sales rep that I was a single mom trying to run a household with three kids and I knew that I had not caused this.

"Yeah, you did," she said with an air of kindness and compassion.

She was right. I'd screwed up. Dealing with the utilities was one of the most basic things I had to do, and I'd forgotten. I felt like such a failure. But just like everyone else, even supermoms stumble. The previous homeowners had left the gas on, giving me two months of leeway. When their account was finally cut off, so was my gas.

All I could think to say to my new BFF at the gas company was, "Do you know what my ex-husband is going to say when my boys tell him that I forgot to turn on the gas? It is going to be the screwup of all screwups!" I was certain that Mr. Former would use this against me. He would say that I managed to pay my bills for my office, but I didn't pay the bills for my family. I prioritized work over the kids. I braced myself for impact. . . .

The Great Distraction

In one of my very first family law cases, my client called me on my mobile phone on a Saturday morning. Her husband was knocking on her door, and she didn't know what to do. I told her she could start by answering the door. To her, a decision that might have once seemed so simple became nearly impossible. She felt threatened, paralyzed, and didn't know how to proceed.

Your initial separation will likely be followed by a similar paralysis—a feeling that you are deep in the trenches of a great period of "stuckness." While there, it will seem as if you can't make any decisions that could shape or impact your future. Interest rates are down, and you can't refinance. You finally sold that old couch on Facebook Marketplace, and you can't decide what to do with the cash. Any impending decisions feel doubly daunting when someone is looking over your shoulder watching your every move, when whatever you say or do is no longer classified.

This is when most of us enter the next stage—the period of Great Distraction. Kitchen reno and new wardrobe, here we come! In my personal life, I tend to ask for forgiveness rather than permission. I also commit and then figure out a way to make my commitment a reality. These characteristics made me a terrible divorce client. I did pretty much everything people told me not to do! My lawyer never would have advised that I buy a new car. Stella, my 1966 Corvette Stingray convertible, was my separation present to myself. But what else is a gal to do when she has finally gotten her groove back? (Thank you to my glam gals who graciously suggested my car's fitting name!)

Truth be told, it's pretty normal to want to buy yourself something special when you separate, but buying a vintage car was not as stereotypical as you might think. See, M.F. insisted that I give him back the orange 1974 Volkswagen Karmann Ghia convertible that he had given to me after I gifted him three wonderful sons. Giving myself Stella felt like I was showing him (and myself) that I could do things on my own. It might not have been the best use of money, but it was what I needed to do for my soul. If buying Stella weren't enough, I also created plenty of other distractions: moving to a new house in the neighborhood, painting every wall, redecorating each room, shopping at consignment stores, opening a new office, and getting my first tattoo. You name it, I turned it into a distraction!

YOU WANT TO FEEL LIKE YOU ARE IN CONTROL OF YOUR FUTURE AND YOUR PRESENT WITHOUT HAVING TO CONTROL EVERY DETAIL EVERY DAY.

The person moving out is usually the person losing power (quite literally, in my case, as the gas fiasco proved). So it's natural to look for and create distractions. You want to feel as if you are still in command of something. The challenge is that these desired distractions come at the very same time stress and scrutiny are increasing in your life, making it nearly impossible to make clear-headed decisions (read: like buying a classic convertible while still figuring out how to pay all your other bills). What's important to accept at this crucial time is that unless you are a professed expert in separation and divorce (which means you've already messed up several times over), *you are going to screw up* or you are going to do something that will be perceived as a screwup! That's the hard, cold truth. Your screwup can be a missed phone call to the gas company or it can be any number of other low-level bad judgment calls (let's hope they are all that simple). Just know that there will always be a list of things that could unintentionally go sideways:

- You might copy your ex on an email intended for a lawyer.

- You might submit an old version of your financial affidavit that doesn't include your new car payment.

- You might miss a deadline or submit a document you forgot to sign.

- You might show up at the wrong place or at the wrong time.

- Your kid may miss practice as you navigate a new carpool and a new group of friends.

- You might not be able to start the lawn mower.

- You might pay your credit card bill (really) late.

- You might pop a tire and not know how to fix it.

- You might go on a date and run into someone you know or sign up for a dating site and find your ex on there.

- You might miss the notice about the nut-free policy at school and pack a peanut butter sandwich in your kid's lunch, only to be sent home the "nut note of shame."

- You might forget Mother's Day, Father's Day, or your own birthday.

Separation adds so much strain that you can feel as if you are losing your mind over everyday decisions that were once so easy to make. Even when it feels as if someone is looking over your shoulder, it's important (for sanity's sake) to let yourself screw up because the compulsion to look over your own shoulder before every decision will quickly become exhausting. Go ahead and forget to turn on the gas. Mistakes are allowed. Just please don't let your screwups ever get as far-fetched as forgetting to pay an escort at a fancy hotel (especially if you live in a State that does not permit dating until your divorce is finalized). While you may be able to do these things legally (or illegally), you may not be able to get out of the damage it does to your credibility.

GOING THROUGH SEPARATION AND DIVORCE MEAN YOU HAVE TO GET COMFORTABLE WITH BEING UNCOMFORTABLE.

Questioning Yourself

I get it. Separation and divorce are new. They're scary. They can be daunting. But you get to decide how you are going to respond. If you've already screwed up or you're swimming in a sea of fear about potentially screwing up, questioning yourself is understandable. But it's important to remember that you still have the capacity to do *whatever you were doing right while you were married*. A superdad's or supermom's wings don't get clipped overnight. Even though it may be difficult for you to see those strengths and abilities in yourself now that you are in the throes of a tumultuous separation, they still exist.

Many years ago, I represented a dad whose wife had made every bad decision she could possibly make. She had hit rock bottom. As the judge essentially stripped the mother of her ability to see her children, the judge told the woman that she hoped this was the bottom and the only place to go from here was up. The separation fog can be truly arduous. But your strength will become clear when you reach the other side. With every step of your separation, you will face choices, many of them difficult ones. Make those choices as best you can. As my girl (and author of *Untamed*), Glennon Doyle said, "I have learned that if I want to rise, I have to sink first."[15] During separation, you may very well sink, but you will also have the choice to rise. Even when your mind teeters and you waiver over different courses of action, you still get to direct the outcome.

The Tough Questions

1. What can you do differently to ensure that you don't keep repeating the same screwups? Can you keep yourself in check by having a friend be your accountability partner?

2. Who can help you evaluate if your screwups are really screwups?

3. What steps can you take or things can you learn to become better organized? Are you willing to do the extra work?

4. Are you open to change in order to navigate your new normal and meet the demands of your daily life?

Technically Speaking

- Never give yourself more than two choices. You won't be able to make bigger decisions if they seem too complicated. In a buffet of options, you will inevitably gorge, blow up, or throw up.

- Give yourself permission to take a break from your separation woes. Do something that inspires you. Some of the best advice I ever received was to take a day off from my separation when I needed it.

- To avoid mess-ups, use two calendars—one for your parenting schedule and kids' activities and a second calendar just for you. You may want to merge or connect your kids' calendar to your smarthome device so they can see it too.

- Set reminders to keep yourself on track and use alarms before the fog sets in. You likely have a smartphone (not a dumb one) and it's yours to use as you please, free of judgment.

- Know that you are inevitably going to have a misstep. I can't promise it will be okay (and that your ex won't use it against you), but you can have compassion for yourself and try to laugh about it when you can.

PART THREE

DIVORCE

IN MANY WAYS, divorce is like New Year's Eve. You've waited for it all year long, you've gotten yourself all done up for the party, and then the ball drops and you realize it's really just another day. Hopefully you didn't spend too much on your outfit or your babysitter!

By definition, divorce is the legal ending of a marriage. But you don't have to be married to *feel like* you are getting divorced. Divorce is as much an emotional thing as a legal one. It is a moment when you are choosing to officially sacrifice your stability and the relationship you once had with the intent of finding a life that is more aligned with your happiness. It is the punctuation mark at the end of the sentence that was your separation. It is also the beginning of a new chapter, a new life.

One of the legal consequence of divorce is that you are free to marry again. Despite misconceptions, divorce may not automatically resolve the issues of asset distribution (who gets what), where the kids are going to be (who gets custody), and how much support someone is going to pay or receive (whether that is child support or alimony). It also does not necessarily mean that the issues you are negotiating, discussing, and trying to resolve with your ex have happened yet. It all depends on the State you are in (the separation period and criteria established for divorce there) and the state you are in (emotionally and in your negotiations).

Ironically, divorce is one of the simplest things that family law attorneys do. While some people may want to continue riding down Separation Street indefinitely (because they don't want to lose health insurance or estate benefits), once the divorce has been filed, you will need to follow the exit signs. When you are served the papers (and the criteria and timeline for divorce are met), you are on cruise control, heading down a one-way street to singledom.

12

It's Going to Suck

Down at Divorcée Café

WHILE LEGAL DIVORCE is heartbreaking for most, it probably won't feel a lot different than when you settled into your separation (if you've gotten there yet). When I first separated, I had to learn how to be alone, which was no small feat for someone carrying around a duffel bag of abandonment issues! I didn't know if I was capable, especially during the weeks when my boys weren't around. To cope, I surrounded myself with community—friends, acquaintances, neighbors, colleagues, and family members. But then it happened: the great reshaping of my social circle and the unexpected shift in friends that divorce precipitates and none of us ever sees coming.

Since my boys didn't have many friends whose parents were separated or divorced (i.e., who didn't live together), my relationships with several of those parents were soon severed. I felt like the outcast. Some of my friends (namely those who were Mr. Former's friends before they became mine, too, and some of my other "couple friends") seemed as confused as I was about their allegiances. Should they stay or should they go now? (Nod to The Clash and those still stuck in the '80s.) Did M.F. tell them they had to choose between us?

Whether it's impromptu or planned, opening yourself up to a social shift takes courage. But it can also be worth the leap. Trust me, I know. In case the purging of my friends (which I had not asked for) wasn't enough, my divorce also raised other unanticipated questions and stresses. There was the time M.F. shared that he wanted to move to Chicago (which meant the children would spend more time in the air than they would just being kids). There was also the first time he didn't return the boys when I thought he would. Solitude seemed unavoidable as I convinced myself I would never see my kids again. I struggled to handle the difficulty of dissolution and its social implication so much so that I considered going back to my marriage many times.[16] But as one of my brothers reminded me, it was too late. Divorce, and any solitude that might come with it, was nearing.

Then one day, I found myself alone, and to my great surprise, I felt strangely at peace. I was still a mom, a business owner, an attorney, a daughter, a sister, and a friend wearing all the same hats, but now I realized I had my very own closet to put them in.

Marriages end in divorce for many reasons. The term *irreconcilable differences* refers to many different scenarios. There are the spouses who realize their partner committed adultery or has an addiction. There is the husband who leaves his wife for someone who was previously a "friend" of the couple. The wife who becomes pregnant after participating in a consensual threesome. The two who grow apart but wait until the children graduate to actually split. Domestic violence and other unresolvable trauma can be definitive factors, too, as can a devastating accident that results in life-changing injuries and a spouse unable to cope under those stresses. The trials and tribulations of divorce are different for every person. Regardless of how it happened or whether you wanted it, there will (and I can't emphasize this enough) *never* be anything normal about divorce. What you will get instead is an experience of substantial change, which 9.9 times out of 10 will suck emotionally and financially.

THERE IS A CERTAIN PAIN AND HUMANITY THAT WEAVES THROUGH ALL DIVORCE CASES.

I've seen it when I tell my clients that it's highly unlikely they will get to spend all of the holidays with their children. Their shoulders invariably slouch, their heads lower, and their hands loosen on the table as I gently nudge the tissue box toward them. The most skilled divorce attorneys will try to tell you what is "normal" in the separation and divorce process, but most will neglect to tell you about the parts that are really going to sting your heart or crush your soul. These "suckness factors" are one of the biggest reasons I wrote this book: to shed light on the "what you don't know" and "what you didn't see coming" aspects of divorce and provide you with empowered choices.

Just because divorce will never be normal

doesn't mean it's not doable. I got through my divorce by prioritizing my support system (my mother and brothers), relying on my friends, and forming a new circle of other divorced moms and dads who were open to carpooling! Down at the local restaurant, fondly referred to as "Divorcée Café" (which, in retrospect, should have been called the "Not Married Market," but more on that later), my circle of fellow newly single friends encouraged me to do the things I had long told my clients to do: create new traditions, celebrate new holidays, and know where to go when you need to socialize with other adults, even if it's somewhere you wouldn't have dared to go alone before!

Challenged by Unintended Consequences

In the 2002 movie *Sweet Home Alabama*, Reese Witherspoon's character, Melanie, reinvents herself, transforming from a small-town Southern girl into a New York City socialite. Having recently become engaged to Andrew, one of the most eligible bachelors in Manhattan, she needs to legally divorce Jake, the hottie back home in Alabama, whom

181

she left after a miscarriage caused them to become estranged. Upon her return home, Melanie struggles to convince Jake to sign the divorce papers. Once he finally surrenders and it appears she is free to marry, her new fiancé Andrew (who is a lawyer) halts the wedding to announce that Melanie never signed the papers. Spoiler alert: she is still in love with Jake.

Once divorce is in motion, it's in motion, and the one thing you can count on is that there will be intended consequences, unintended consequences, and some stigmas you never saw coming your way. You might think that things are going to be different once you are divorced. But while things may *feel* different, your relationship with your ex and kids could be the same, or it could be worse, depending on the other humans involved and the state they are in. My advice to you (no matter what the circumstances) is this: don't assume the worst, but at the same time, be prepared for it. So many things go into severing a relationship with your spouse and beginning a new type of relationship with your children. But here's what you can count on happening:

- You become officially "unmarried" and are legally able to wed someone else, should you so choose.

- Unlike *Sweet Home Alabama*'s Melanie, you likely won't move back home to be with your ex.

- Your money becomes *your* money (which also means you must begin building credit if you haven't already done so).

- You check a new box on the "marital status" section of intake forms.

- You no longer have to ask permission to paint the walls.

And here are some of the things you wouldn't have seen coming:

- Your friends will change, and, if you have more than one kiddo, the great carpool shuffle will become a standard experience.

- Your health insurance eligibility or availability may change.

- You may have to get new car insurance.

- You may have to file taxes differently or by yourself for the first time.

- Your values and priorities might be challenged. For example, you may have assured your high school graduate that you would help with college expenses. Now that you are separated and divorced, those funds may need to be paid to your soon-to-be ex or you. Unless there is an agreement or court order to the contrary, grown children's expenses cannot be prioritized over financial support for a dependent spouse.

- You may have to celebrate new holidays, or holidays in a new way. *Yes Day*? (While *Yes Day* was a movie released in 2021, starring Jennifer Garner, it can also be a fun replacement holiday for a missed birthday!)

- Your estate rights and inheritances will change (be sure to update all relevant paperwork on your end as well).

- If you own a company, many companies have dissolution triggers in the event one of the partners divorces. Check your agreement.

- If you share liability with your ex, a creditor doesn't care. They just want to be paid. If you left out a debt when you resolved your case and they want their money, they're coming after you!

- Health-care providers may also have the right to collect on any outstanding balances related to your spouse (it's part of the Doctrine of Necessaries in some States, which also holds you liable for necessary support for your children).

ONCE THE DIVORCE TRAIN IS IN MOTION, THERE MAY BE NO STOPS ON THE RIDE.

There are a lot of unknowns at this juncture of your separation and divorce, but one thing remains clear: when it comes to the entry of a divorce judgment, you have no other option but to sign the divorce papers. (Notice, I am not referencing any of the other big issues such as custody, support, alimony, and the division of assets and debts. Ideally, these should already be resolved by the time you put pen to paper.) But most people are wholly unprepared for this moment because they didn't know what things would look like on the other side of divorce. You have to be able to take a balcony view of the situation before you ever get to this stage and know how your decisions will impact you, your family, your work, and your friends. Don't be afraid to ask questions early in the process about what can happen. Be proactive in finding out things up front. Talk to a lawyer to understand what divorce means in your State and how you can ensure that everything that needs to be resolved before this turning point gets resolved.

Sticking It to the Stigmas

Even when you think that all the technical details of divorce have been addressed, society can still surprise you. I was recently completing an intake form at my new family doctor's office when I was stopped cold by a question at the bottom of the page. *Relationship status: single, married, separated, divorced, or widowed.* Why? What did they care? They already had my health insurance and my emergency contact, so what business of theirs was my relationship status? What did they have to gain by knowing? And would checking the box for *separated, divorced,* or *widowed* mean that they would be concerned for my emotional well-being? *Please don't tell me there will be a slew of sorries coming my way. . . .*

The form was otherwise exceptionally current, containing an exhaustive list of sexual orientations and pronoun preferences. So where were the other status boxes—like the one for the unmarried business owner, lawyer, and mother of three with a dog side-kick? Where were the options for common law or consciously uncoupled? Maybe Katherine Woodward Thomas (author of the *New York Times* best-seller *Conscious Uncoupling: 5 Steps to Living Happily* Even *After*) could help! I wanted so badly to pick up a bright crayon off the kids' table and color in a big red flag next to my own little box that said "not married."

With divorce, often one of the biggest unintended consequences is the possibility of giving up the stability and respect in your community (automatically extended to you as a married human) in exchange for a label (plus, of course, a life that is better aligned with what you really want). You see it on all kinds of forms and hear it in people's whispers. It has even happened to me while sitting at football games. Two moms in front of me were talking loud enough for the rest of the fans to hear. One of them asked if the person in question lived over at the new apartment complex on the west side because that's where the divorced people live. I paused. *Breathe*, I thought to myself. "Oh, you mean the happy people? The people who are living their best life?" I laughed but my heart ached. It ached not only for the new stigma attached to my boys and me, but it also ached for the parent who didn't choose divorce. What about them? What about the parent who was in an abusive marriage or the parent who doesn't feel like they can leave because they can't afford to live alone?

HOW IS IT THAT SOMETHING SO COMMONPLACE REMAINS SO TABOO?

In today's modern society, where in the US alone nearly 750,000 marriages end in divorce or annulment annually,[17] why is divorce not respected as something more commonplace? Divorcées are labeled as *outcast*s, thought of as *broken* or *available*, and generally looked down upon. You name it, people will call you it or think it. You may still be an amazing parent and human being, but when you get divorced, you're slapped with labels you never asked for—all because it turns out that you, your ex, or both of you weren't amazing partners for each other. Divorce is either going to be the bottom of the roller coaster of grief or the top on the roller coaster of freedom. Some days (or minutes) it may feel like both.

The Tough Questions

1. How do you respond to your Mr. or Mrs. Former's shit-talking, oversharing, or outright attempts to highjack your friend groups?

2. What are your coping mechanisms? Are they healthy and going to help you transition successfully into your new life?

3. How will you deal with your partner's new love interest (especially if that person is someone you believe was the impetus for your split)?

4. Do you understand projection and how it is impacting you? (For instance, when Human A, who is a classic narcissist, accuses Human B of ruining their life, but it is actually Human A who is ruining Human B's life.) Kettle black? Some people believe that in such

situations, narcissists are often just telling on themselves. Are you Human A or Human B? Even without a personality disorder, projection can happen to anyone.

Technically Speaking

- Join a women's or men's group supporting those going through divorce.

- Start a text thread or Facebook group with others who are also experiencing divorce or can give you tips as you craft your new normal.

- Write down what you want to get in your divorce. Peace is an acceptable answer but not the only thing you need.

- Narrow down your desired goals, focusing on your priorities. When it comes time to talk about what you want, is Christmas or your holiday season more important than your family's annual reunion? Is liquidity more important than adding to your retirement funds? How important is where your children attend school? Do you want to be responsible for the family home and all the related expenses on your new single-income budget?

13

More Resolution Options than New Year's Eve

Mr. Smells Good

MR. SMELLS GOOD was a retired professional athlete. When he walked into the firm, he was in his forties and owned several businesses. He and his wife had been together since the start of his athletic career. Both were actively involved in their children's lives, and both were trying to find a way to make themselves financially whole post-divorce. However, they were used to a lifestyle that would be difficult to maintain individually.

By the time Mr. S.G. came to our office, he was disabled and couldn't play anymore. His wife, who had not worked full-time in years, expected half of their retirement savings. Given that both spouses were in good communication, we attempted to resolve their differences outside of court. They each had attorneys, and we chose a solid mediator. When the mediator finally joined the proceedings (after spending three hours with the wife discussing her needs in the negotiation), my client immediately grabbed three of his fingers and snapped them to the side. They resembled a contorted version of the Vulcan salutation from *Star Trek*.

"Can my wife do this?" he grumbled. It was eerie, but he made his point. After decades on the sports field (which earned them a lifestyle that most could only dream about), his fingers were stuck sideways. He lived in pain and discomfort, and he wanted to make it clear that he would never be able to work again. He needed his wife to help with her own future and not rely only on the savings he had contributed to. Mr. Smells Good explained his position to the mediator, stating that the reason they had very healthy retirement accounts was because he had been willing to sacrifice his body, his brain, and years of his life on the field.

The perception of most spouses is that they

worked together to put the money away for retirement so they don't understand why that money would no longer be there for them when they need it. According to that logic, the partner who was the wage earner has an ability to continue to add to their half of the pie. But as this scenario proves, that's not always the case. My client wanted to do the right thing, but he didn't want to be taken advantage of. Ultimately, we had to follow the law in our State, which requires that an estate be divided equitably (based on the monetary values agreed upon), even though there was only one working person in the marriage. Mr. Smells Good and his ex-wife were able to work out a resolution (though not without some *Star Trek* power and patience).

WHEN IT COMES TO FINANCIAL SUPPORT, THERE IS NO ONE-SIZE-FITS-ALL SOLUTION.

If you're the party who ends up having to provide financial support to your spouse, you'll always think that you are paying them way too much. If you are the person receiving financial support, you'll never feel as if you're getting enough. Except in the case of the successful retired pro athlete who maintained an amicable relationship with his ex, former spouses stretching one or two incomes across two households typically find it difficult to live the same lifestyle they did before they separated. When it comes to financial support based on income versus assets (whether it is paid monthly or in a lump sum), there is no one-size-fits-all equation, even when certain States have calculators. Ultimately, most families have to make a decision as to *how* (not *if*) they are going to adjust their lifestyles.

You've Got Options, but Not Paying Isn't Likely One of Them

On an almost daily basis, I am asked how much divorce will cost. Tongue in cheek, I answer, "How much money do you have?" On the way from Charlotte to Atlanta, I once saw a giant billboard with a picture of a very gentle-looking, fortysomething woman promoting "Simple Divorces" for $500. I am calling *1-800-0-CHANCE*. An amount of $500 may begin to cover the cost of legally ending your marriage,

194

but it is not going to cover all the time it will take to resolve who's going to get what, pay for what, and have the kids when. A courtroom case is going to be the most expensive route, and if you hire a lawyer who is unwilling to resolve things or who does not respond on a timely basis, the process will quickly become an expensive marathon. Outside the courtroom (or mediation if that's the way you go), there will be other fees associated with alimony, asset distribution, and child support. In most States, things will just come down to whether there is enough money to go around.

When it comes to finalizing the decisions of divorce, you have several resolution options:

1. RESOLVE IT ON YOUR OWN

When it came to settling my own divorce, I was adamant about handling our resolution outside the courtroom. I told Mr. Former that he could have whatever he wanted other than us getting back together. At least once a week, if I tell someone my story about wanting to resolve things outside of Court (and privately), they will ask me what I did that was so bad. Did I take his money? Did I have multiple affairs? Was there abuse? Was I trying to run away and join the circus? No. No. I had enough of a circus right at home, thanks! I wanted to keep our children, our families, and our work life free from the conflict between us. And I wanted it over then . . . not several difficult, angry, and complicated years later.

If you and your spouse are equally unhappy and parting amicably, you may try to resolve things on your own. You will save a lot in attorney fees and likely will not have future (high) conflict situations, but you also won't know what you don't know! If you do it completely by yourselves, you may not get a good look at the whole picture, and you may miss something that you have to do or you need to discuss. You both must also be willing to compromise. Then once you have arrived at an agreement, you'll want to have it reviewed and drafted by a lawyer and executed properly.

2. MEDIATION

In most divorce cases, spouses are required to attend mediation as an alternative form of resolution before letting the Court decide for you. For some, it can be a primary resolution choice. Mediation is a hurry-up-and-wait process though (so bring a book or your laptop!). A neutral party (typically an attorney and preferably one who practices family law) follows a standard procedure to help you reach an agreement. Some mediators may even be non-attorneys (such as mental health workers or clergy members). In any case, you'll have to have the terms of your agreement legally drafted by a lawyer to close the gaps on what you may have missed or not known.

Mediation can occur with or without legal counsel, and even when there is pending litigation. Opening statements may be presented in the initial session, after which both parties (and their respective counsels if present) separate into different rooms while the mediator meets alternately with them. If you both walk out of the mediation process unhappy and with an agreement, then it was a success because it means you both compromised to reach that agreement. If you aren't willing to compromise, all you are doing is paying a very expensive babysitter! You won't always be able to settle issues against the other human in the other room and changes in financial positions aren't always going to be disclosed. Mediation will last as long as you give it. If you say it will be done in four hours, it will. If you give it seventeen hours, it will likely take that long (yes, I've been there). Pack a lunch, order pizza, and be prepared.

A good mediator can play and understand both sides. Former judges make great mediators because they'll be very real with you about what may happen in the courtroom if you have to go there. It can change the course of your negotiation when you hear: "No, a judge would not allow you to have 75 percent of the estate. They will also not tell you that you have to pay all the debt and remove yourself from your children's lives."

3. ARBITRATION

Arbitration is like mediation, except that at the end, the arbitrator (a lawyer) makes the final decision (which may be referred to as the Arbitrator's Award or ruling). If you don't like what was decided, there is a process by which you can appeal the decision. The proceeding is similar to a courtroom proceeding, but it is often held in a conference room at one of the lawyer's offices with a court reporter present. You will go through the discovery process (the exchanging of evidence) and the presentation of testimony by all the witnesses, then the arbitrator will make a decision (the ruling or award). In both mediation and arbitration, you exchange information that supports the claims you filed. Caution: it may be that all the information provided is not all the information that exists. You can agree on how much time will be allotted for your case to be heard by the arbitrator, but the longer the proceedings go, the greater your financial burden. You might also be paying a panel of arbitrators (who all bill by hourly clocks).

A handshake will not be enough to ensure the terms of your arbitration agreement; a legal document will need to be drafted reflecting the terms of resolution. You'll want a good lawyer by your side because your lawyer becomes your voice. Who you choose determines how well your story will be told, regardless of your selected path to resolution. Ensure that your lawyer can read a room and knows the law (which may sound obvious but is not). Experience matters, but ultimately, how well they know the law and how your story gets communicated depend on who that communicator is as a human being. Yes, lawyers are human, and not all lawyers are created equal.

4. LITIGATION

Litigation is when the Court decides. It can also be a very expensive story time. In court you have little control over how long things will go or how much time you will have to present the case. Even if you are given ample time, "your day in court" will never be exactly what you expected, and your property will not magically and easily be divided. There will never be enough time to tell your story, nor will there be enough time to refute every point or summarize a five-, ten-, or twenty-year marriage. Your lawyers will take the best facts you have to support the argument and present those to the judge. That means many things will go unsaid.

On top of contending with a very busy court-room calendar, there are plenty of delay tactics that can turn the divorce marathon into an ultramar-athon. If your opponent sees that you are getting too much traction, they will try to freeze you out like a tennis partner who is up 30-Love. (A popular tactic is going for a never-ending bath-room break.) There are also some hard truths that you have to be prepared to manage with litigation. One such truth is that people lie under oath on the witness stand. Is that your surprised face? I sure was stunned when a witness lied during my first ever domestic violence proceeding where I was representing the victim.

Often divorce pleadings and processes involve stressful time restrictions and some very damaging allegations (everything from details of your financial woes to the name you called your spouse during a heated argument five years ago). Almost nothing is off the table, and once you have verified a pleading, it's like casting your vote: you can't take it back. Ultimately, litigation can feel like a full season (or two) of *Survivor* rolled up into just a few days.

People often choose court or arbitration because they don't want to be the one to make the decision. They want someone to tell them what to do, or they don't want the other spouse to resent them for making the decision independently. Some choose court because they think their case is so strong they will get to see their partner hurt or reprimanded in a public capacity. You'll likely end up further away from reaching your prioritized goals because you put the decision for your family and yourself in the hands of someone else—someone who only sees and hears you in an antagonistic and stressful environment. And for the record, bringing your children to the courtroom rarely helps a judge, the children, or your family.

DIVORCE CAN FEEL LIKE TRYING TO SPRINT IN STILETTOS.

In any resolution form, divorce is never going to be lightning fast. It's not going to happen like a quickie marriage at an Elvis wedding chapel in Vegas. Don't expect to go in on a Monday and be done by Wednesday, even if you live in a small town and know the judge. Ask your attorney about ranges of costs and a timeline of events, then ask for updates along the way. Things change. New evidence is discovered. Global pandemics can close down all legal proceedings.

I've described divorce as a marathon, though some might say it's a *triathlon*. As in try, try, try as you might, it's going to feel like another full-time job (on top of the other one, two, or five you already have). Know that after you choose your course of resolution, there will be unexpected hurdles. Having realistic expectations will help you clear them. No matter what resolution track you choose, divorce will take great preparation and persistence, but the process doesn't have to crush your spirit. If it helps ease the way just a bit, you can remind yourself that whatever you must do, the "other side" has to do it too!

The Tough Questions

1. Knowing your spouse, what is the best resolution option for you? As you try to figure that out, ask yourself: What will be the most intimidating route? What will be the easiest?

2. What amount are you willing to spend for your resolution option? And what is more important to you, time or money?

3. How much time will be allotted to your case if you use the court system? Will it be enough?

4. When you feel as if you have to defend yourself, are you arguing on principle?

5. How do you feel about alimony or child support? Do you understand how it works and how or why it can be terminated?

Technically Speaking

- Understand the basic proceedings of divorce before you get started. At our firm, the divorce process is broken into four phases (known as "The Sodoma Way"):

  1. Initial Call & Consultation
  2. Contract & Discovery
  3. Resolution, Litigation & Final Documents
  4. Closing of the File

- It's amazing how often a client will "forget" they have an asset and not disclose it. It is critical that you disclose your assets or that you ensure there is a provision that speaks to a waiver of disclosure. It is also crucial to know if there is a penalty for failure to disclose and what that penalty is.

- Start organizing all things related to your finances. Create a balance sheet and financial budget that reflects your past, current, and anticipated expenses. (Still feeling new to numbers of all kinds? Check out videos and resources from some of the respected financial teachers mentioned earlier in the book: Jean Chatzky, Dave Ramsey, Napoleon Hill, David Bach, and Robert Kiyosaki.)

- Have your attorney help you hire a financial planner who can support you in understanding your financial needs and expenses for the future. From there, you can decide what's important to you in terms of where your money goes.

- Find out about the background and experience of the mediator, arbitrator, or judge assigned to your case.

- Locate and review all your life insurance and retirement policies to identify beneficiaries. Change them where they need to be changed.

- For some peace of mind, you might want to spend some quality time reading *The Good Divorce*, a book by late psychologist and former Director of the Family Therapy Doctoral Training Program at USC, Dr. Constance Ahrons. After divorcing twice and spending three decades helping other families cope with marriage dissolution, Dr. Ahrons coined the term "binuclear family" and was an early champion of collaborative divorce.

14

Sometimes Wins Won't Feel Like Wins

JUST LIKE SO MANY of my peers, on the day of graduation from law school I held my JD (Juris Doctor) degree (which could also stand for "Just" about any "Direction") and wondered what area of law I would ultimately practice. As a young adult, my biggest dream was to be a sports entertainment lawyer. I loved sports, journalism, writing, and all things communication. But it's clear to me now, given the events of my childhood and my parents' "irreconcilable differences," I was destined to be a divorce attorney. It just took a few twists and turns to get there.

My first "real" job offer while I was attending law school was in Chicago. Had I taken that position, I would have been negotiating contracts between athletes and big brands like Kellogg's. It sounded ideal to me, but it smelled like an internship, and not having a regular income while I was racking up tuition debt made it a no-go. So I made a list of five law firms in Charlotte that both interested me and held some personal connection. Then I started dialing. Beginning with number five on the list, I met one of the partners for lunch and got the job later that afternoon. I was told that I would be working in business law, creating start-ups, negotiating commercial leases, and assisting in commercial real estate transactions. What my new boss failed to disclose up front was that he also represented a multitude of strip clubs and sex shops. His way of telling me was by saying, "Hey, Nic, you okay with vibrators?"

How exactly does one answer such a question? "Yeah, they've always worked just fine? I especially like the [fill in the absurd vibrator brand name here]. It really does the trick." Apparently, my boss's former paralegal had trouble with the mention of sex toys whenever he dictated letters for her to transcribe. I wonder why. Frankly, I was keen to have a good job, so I politely told him that vibrators would be no problem. What I didn't realize was the bigger picture at play.

It wasn't long before my new boss had me visiting the sex shops and managing a zoning violation for one of the strip clubs. Whereas I once pictured myself working in a big office tower, wearing my black power suit, and doing a kick-ass job, I was sent to a rather unexpected place of business and told to blend in as I discretely monitored "jobs" of a very different kind. Note to the curious reader: strip clubs are vastly different experiences when you visit them at lunch and again at midnight.

A WIN IS AN INTERESTING THING TO DEFINE, ESPECIALLY IN DIVORCE.

Was my new job a win? Would it be a *real* win if I helped the sex shop come out "ahead"? A win is an interesting thing to define, especially in divorce. Twentysomething years into my career as a divorce attorney, when people ask me how many cases I've won, I usually laugh out loud. Even when you are fighting for what you believe is right, sometimes wins won't feel like wins at all. It's how you define a win. In the family law arena, things are so unpredictable and stressful. Sometimes how you look at and approach the issues are what make the biggest difference in the outcome.

Sole Custody Won't Cut It

"I want sole custody" is a statement I hear often when it comes to desired wins, but so rarely is it a realistic outcome. In some courtrooms, you will be reprimanded for even mentioning the word "sole." Is sole custody (also referred to as "full custody") really a win? Or is shared custody the real win for your kids? And if you don't win, will you appeal? If you decide to appeal the decision, be forewarned: it could be a multiyear struggle to get what you want, and what you want may change over time. This is not to dissuade you but rather to help set expectations for you in your crusade.

If custody is in conflict, it is important to know that both parents have equal rights to their children; there is no presumption that one parent is better than the other. In a custody claim, there are a wide variety of factors the Court must consider before making a determination about what is in the best interest and welfare of the child. Among those considerations are the mental and physical health of each parent and of their child. Logistics are also considered: Does either parent have to travel for work? Does the child have an illnesses or high needs? The list is endless. Parenting scheduling is also endless, but the great majority of cases will *not* result in 365 days for one parent and 0 for the other. In some States, there is a minimum custody schedule that guarantees both parents have time. In others, there are shared schedules, such as a week on and a week off or a 2-2-5 arrangement (where the children spend two days with each parent and then five days with each parent). Too confusing? Don't worry, there is also the 2-2-3 parenting schedule (two days with one parent, two days with the other parent, and three days with the first parent, switching roles the next week to balance things out). Again, there is no one-size-fits-all solution, and the State you live in matters.

SOMETIMES YOU HAVE TO REDEFINE SUCCESS.

All this is to say that you need to be realistic about your expectations and outcomes (and simplify wherever you can). In custody cases, just as in divorce proceedings, even if you win one issue, you'll probably lose another. In our society we think success means winning it all, but sometimes you have to lose one issue (and accept that you gave it your best) to emerge victorious. There are times when you must redefine success by considering what the outcome is going to feel like and how it will impact your family, rather than what it is going to look like to other people.

Wronging Our Rights

Picture a football game (the "all-American" kind). The field is filled with passion for the win. And throughout the game, the wide receiver and a defensive back have been going at it. The defensive back punches the wide receiver over and over when no one is looking. The wide receiver finally has enough and crushes the defensive back, right in front of the referee. A flag is thrown. The wide receiver is the only player penalized. No one noticed the prodding, trash talking, or the punches thrown by the defensive back ever since the start of the game. The moral of the story is that if you're always on the defensive and focused on the back-and-forth jabs, you won't get the touchdown you're fighting for. Not only will resentment build with each punch but the accumulation of jabs will ultimately result in a response that is far greater than any individual blow (like a muscular wide receiver coming at you full throttle). Conflict increases when one player feels blindsided and all the punches thrown his way are absorbed without any response but not without impact.

When I split from Mr. Former, it was because I didn't want to be in a marriage with someone I'd stopped liking and someone who didn't seem to like me. Then I got stuck dealing with an even less likeable human in divorce. Sometimes, if you are the spouse who didn't want the divorce, you may have to learn how to "unlike" your partner (unless it's a super emotionally mature partnership where you can communicate with each other and get along throughout your separation). From my experience working with thousands of partners, it's an anomaly when two people who have children together get along well post-separation. Some may dislike their spouse more than they like their children. However, there is a difference between disliking someone and constantly trash talking or throwing jabs at them. In divorce cases (and battles), no matter how fiercely you keep your head down or fists up, you're never going to get exactly what you want.

You have to decide what is enough. Revenge, for instance, might be sweet, but it will never be sweet enough. And if you think that a big fat alimony check will make things better, think again. If you are the receiving spouse, can you count on the money? Do you really want to be tiptoeing around potential termination triggers that would end your financial support? Seeking alimony from a supporting spouse with a drug habit they can't kick or one who is sleeping with an office colleague could result in alimony ending when they lose their job or find themselves in rehab. Is it worth the risk? If you're living in a State with laws like North Carolina, you'll need to think long and hard about living with someone else or remarrying because you may lose your alimony. ("Cohabitating" is also a legal term of art, in case you want to tack on more time in court fighting that one.)

THERE IS A WAY OUT, AND IT DOESN'T HAVE TO BE A FIGHT TO GET THERE.

As a divorce attorney, I'm a fierce advocate for my clients. I'm also a human who recognizes the darkness, devastation, and discombobulation that come with divorce. I know there is a way out, and it doesn't have to be a fight. Your best strategy for success is always going to be staying on the offensive (just like Mr. Out of State and his fishbowl of bubblegum). If you are constantly swinging, you will likely go down swinging, which is not a good look on anyone. You *can* find a way to share life with your ex, participate in experiences, and lift each other up for the sake of the children, but you're going to have to love the children more than you hate each other. It is going to require work, support, and understanding. And none of this happens easily on or off the field on game day.

The Tough Questions

1. What does success look like to you? Regarding the custody arrangement you are seeking, is it for your own and your family's benefit? Or is it for how it will appear to others?

2. What level of satisfaction, liberation, or happiness would lead you to feel successful?

3. What can you control in your pursuit of success?

4. Write down five things hindering your working on a respectful parenting partnership with your ex. It would help if your list doesn't look like this:

   - *They are a narcissist.*
   - *They are a narcissist.*
   - *They are a narcissist.*
   - *They are a narcissist.*
   - *They are a narcissist.*

Technically Speaking

- Create a list of goals at the beginning of your case. Review it every three months.

- Some jurisdictions require that all parents who file litigation participate in a course on co-parenting. Co-parenting is only as good as the parents' willingness to participate in the fundamentals.

- Parenting coordinators may be available in your jurisdiction. These are neutral parties who have received certifications to help parents in high-conflict custody cases communicate more effectively so the children's needs remain the priority.

- If you are seeking a new custody schedule, track your child/children's grades as well as their attendance and tardy records to help determine whether the schedule you are seeking will be better or worse than the schedule currently in place. These records may also be helpful to the Court.

15

The "Divorce Diet" Is Real!

The Disheveled Divorcée

WHEN "DEEDEE," the Disheveled Divorcée, walked into our office, she was a disaster. She was an inherently beautiful thirtysomething, but she looked terribly rundown. Her hair was untamed, her skin pale, and her cheeks sunken. She hadn't been the one to initiate the end of her marriage, and she remained a stay-at-home mom now living in an overpriced shithole with her elementary school-aged daughter. After her separation, she had gotten the only apartment she could, but it was full of mold and gravely affecting her health. Her home environment mirrored the toxicity of her divorce proceedings.

When you get divorced, you recognize the

finality of it all. One of the hardest things to figure out when you have "arrived" are the finances. This is especially true if you've never been involved with household expenses, haven't worked during your marriage, or you've never built credit for yourself. Deedee was in that boat, without a paddle. She wasn't in a good place financially or emotionally. With every meeting we had, I watched her get thinner and thinner. She went from lean to emaciated.

As an attorney there to help her start a new life (not end her marriage), I called around to my contacts who managed apartment complexes. I gave them her budget, asked them to provide her with two options, and arranged for them to show her the properties at 4 p.m. the following Thursday. Deedee was exhausted (this is not something that goes away once you're divorced), so I wanted to do everything possible to give her a new solid foundation from which to rise. Within a matter of days we found her and her daughter a clean, modern apartment with airy colors, a simple design, and lots of sunshine. A year later, after her case was resolved, she walked into our office, and I hardly recognized her. Her hair was glistening and she looked healthy and physically fit. She was also wearing a shirt that read *Let that shit go*.

From where I sit as a divorce attorney, I can tell you that there will always be a physical and mental impact to divorce. But not every lawyer is equipped to support both. In fact, when Deedee lost so much weight, opposing counsel attributed the loss to her mental health and started to attack her parenting skills. It became such a crazy conversation that I almost started believing it. Then when I separated, I, too, stopped eating without even noticing it, until I reached the point where my pants were hanging off me. I realized that the Divorce Diet is real, and I wasn't alone! The *New York Times*, the *Seattle Times*, and even country superstar Blake Shelton[18] (after his split from Miranda Lambert) have reported on it. It's common while going through divorce to be unable to keep food down. Sometimes people have no appetite at all or eating is simply an afterthought, as evidenced by an article on the *TODAY* show website, "Divorce Diet: When Slimming Down after Splitting Up Isn't a Good Thing."[19] Further to this point, a 2003 Cornell University study revealed that "sociodemographic variables, including marital change, were more predictive of variation in weight loss than weight gain."[20]

Most of the time, there's nothing "wrong with you," you're just going through divorce!

It's hard not to worry about clients who lose so much weight as they drop to the bottom of the roller coaster of grief. But more often than not, the loss is simply attributable to divorce. The truth for many, though, is that despite all the mental, emotional, and financial strain you will feel, divorce may end up looking great on you. A glass-half-full attitude may help you see it as an opportunity to create a healthy new lifestyle. (You can borrow my rose-colored glasses if you're doubtful.)

The Emotional Duress of Divorce

While divorce can be an unintentional way to lose weight (arguably more effective than any intentional New Year's resolutions to diet), the loss can have some not-so-appealing consequences. It can force flare-ups of other underlying health conditions, prompt the return of illnesses such as cancer, or manifest in you literally pulling out your hair or eyebrows, as it did for a few of my clients. If you find yourself on the Divorce Diet, I caution you to look at *what you are replacing food with.*

One question I often ask clients in my consults is: *What medications are you taking and who prescribes them?* What I'm looking for is prescriptions from multiple pharmacies, physician's notes, and any possible issues that are likely to manifest during the dispute. Alcohol use or alcoholism is a common topic raised in divorce cases. As one of my judges put it, "I'm giving you a choice, alcohol or your children. If you can't decide, then you have a problem with alcohol." There are many ways to address alcoholism in court orders (not all of which you will like if you are the one with the problem), but none of them mean you will necessarily lose your kids.

Most often, situations of strain or turning to substances directly relate to the stress and emotional duress faced in divorce. A 2021 University of Copenhagen study found that recent divorcees and those involved in higher-conflict divorces had significantly higher perceived stress levels.[21] Any divorce will carry with it a burden of stress and the likely loss of weight. When it comes to the strains of divorce and the side effects thereof, it's important to be fully present and ask the right questions.

For so long mental illness has been a top taboo topic, right up there with divorce. When the two collide, the need to have compassion becomes critical. If you're struggling, talk to someone. If someone comes to you for help, listen. Otherwise, accusations may be made, and you may find yourself carrying a fishbowl with 180 pieces of bubblegum into the courtroom to try to prove your innocence.

Like a visit to the dark caves of Runaway Mountain at Six Flags Over Texas, the emotional roller coaster of divorce will inevitably take you through the tunnel. You just don't want to stay in there too long (or give in to too many vices while lingering in its depths). Sometimes you won't realize what you are feeling. Divorce should be a time to turn toward what you are emotionally managing rather than away from it. Let yourself be in the ups, the downs, and all the places in between. Feel the pain. Have the emotion. Then find your way out of the tunnel.

Awareness and Self-Advocacy

Global singing sensation Adele said she had the most terrifying anxiety attacks after leaving her marriage. She was aware of it happening, but she felt as if she had no control over her body. Exhaustion had taken over as she tried to get through the divorce process, be a single parent, deal with not seeing her son every single day, and also run a home and a business. She felt like not doing it anymore, but she also wanted to move forward with intention. To find progress in the process, she set a daily 9 a.m. date with her trusted personal trainer. She didn't intend to lose weight, but she said that exercising helped her "get her mind right" and gave her real purpose.

DIVORCE CAN FEEL LIKE A GUT PUNCH, BUT DON'T LET IT KNOCK YOU DOWN.

Recognize the devastation and darkness in the situation, but also see the light and know there is a way out. While you likely won't regain any weight during the process, divorce should ultimately be a story about you regaining independence. People who haven't been through it won't necessarily understand what you are experiencing, nor should you expect them to. Since you can't control others, you must retrain your response to your situation, keeping your eye on the end results. Time on its own will not heal the loss. Only you will. And it's going to take reflection and some serious self-work.

As I've said before, living through divorce comes down to choice—the very reason this book was written. You get to decide what you want to do to get to the place where you begin again. Surround yourself with people who can speak to you with that "warrior spirit" and help you see things from an offensive perspective. Find the right resources, friends, communities, and legal representation for *you*—those who understand the space you are in.

Just like you will eventually regain your footing after stepping off the Six Flags coaster and feeling very wobbly legged, you will regain your balance after divorce. And much like the lunch you mistakenly ate before boarding the ride, things are simply shifting around inside you. In time, all will settle. You will come out the other side of the mountain. Stay positive. Stay present. Embrace the learning and the growth. You might not be able to control the next turn things take, but you will always be in control of you and your response to it! The best thing you can do is maintain (self) awareness and recognize how things are changing for you. Check in with your body and keep your mental health "top of mind." Prepare yourself emotionally for what will follow the finale (the finality of being unmarried). And remember that your lawyer is not there to teach you how to reshape your responses and build self-advocacy. Well, they might be. But it will be a *very* expensive learning journey if you lean on them for everything (and the results will likely be temporary, as your lawyer is not your therapist). So step up to your personal power shoes and own that stance.

The Tough Questions

1. Stop and take note of your body, how you feel, and what you ate today. Have you unintentionally stopped eating because of stress?

2. If you have stopped eating, what are you replacing food with?

3. What are you doing to help change your stress response and raise yourself up?

4. Who is supporting you through the process?

5. What are your coping mechanisms when faced with stress?

Technically Speaking

- If meditation is not your thing, consider *active meditation* instead. Spend time understanding your brain chemistry and what it takes for you to get from an emotional low to an emotional higher ground.

- Engage with the right professionals to help you manage the stress that divorce may create in your body and mind. Make sure they are properly accredited and a good fit for your style and needs.

- If you're someone who is not comfortable talking about emotions (or you don't know how to accurately describe them), find or create games to make it easier to identify the emotion you are feeling. Perhaps you create "yes," "no," and "maybe" piles for particular emotions that a therapist or friend asks you whether you are feeling.

- Need a little extra pick-me-up . . . or some voices of reason whispering in your ear? Check out Emily and Amelia Nagoski's book *Burnout: The Secret to Unlocking the Stress Cycle*. Or take advantage of the resources at The American Institute of Stress (https://www. stress.org).

16

Today Is the First Day of the Rest of Your Life

CALL ME CRAZY, but during the writing of this book, I got engaged to be married *again*. That's right, the marriage-loving divorce attorney went ahead and got engaged while writing a book about divorce. Oh, the sweet irony. I'm back on the upswing of the roller coaster of grief and freedom, relieved to be hearing "congratulations" instead of "sorry."

My person, George, was referred to me as a divorce client by a business banker (one we shared in common without knowing it). When he walked into our office, he had an undeniable swagger but humble eyes. So that I could focus on what was important (him), I brought another attorney to our conference room and let her take the wheel. A month later, George sent me an email after realizing that we not only had the same banker, but we also had a business consultant and several friends in common. He asked me to join him for a bike ride and dinner. Feeling overly anxious about our first date, I decided to surprise him by casually stopping by his place the night before. While I hoped he might appreciate my spontaneity, I actually wanted to make sure I was ready to go on an official date. Call it a trial run—as in, if it didn't feel right, I would run! When I saw George that night, his swagger, humble eyes, and bright smile drew me in even more, leading me to feel close to him in an unexplainable way. We have seen each other every day since that night.

George planned his proposal after talking with my boys. I had asked him to stay over one Friday evening so he could help with the carpools the next morning. He was up early to go for a bike ride before the chaos of the kids' game day began. I thought he had hit the road already when my two youngest kids climbed into bed and started acting *far* too nice. They were saying things such as, "Aren't we the best teddy bears ever?" I begged them to let me sleep longer and rolled over. When my eyes opened,

George had his arm outstretched and said he needed to ask me a question. He pulled me out of bed and got on one knee (which means I could actually see him eye-to-eye, because he's 6'8" and I'm 5'3"). He said a whole bunch of really amazing things to me, none of which I remembered after the words fell from his lips, and then a whole bunch more to the boys. He proposed, and I said yes. I was in shock. I could hardly believe that I was going to jump on the marriage train yet again. But George is an incredible human, and if I am going to do it all over again, it definitely will be with him.

LOOKING BACK WITH FOND MEMORIES CAN HELP YOU MOVE FORWARD IN A POSITIVE NEW WAY.

After we got engaged, I had the feeling that one of my boys might not want to come to our wedding. Whether it was because he felt like he was losing me, or he felt as if participating would somehow be disloyal to his dad, or he was just feeling crummy that afternoon, his response hit me hard. I sat in my car trying to process what it might be like for any child to go through the ordeal of seeing your parents divorce and then each remarry.

Repressed memories started to surface. I recalled being at my father's wedding as a teenager. He married the woman from the big picture window in our old house—a woman not much older than my eldest brother. None of us liked her, and there were so many reasons why! I remember thinking that if my father had worked at a gas station, she probably wouldn't have looked at him twice. While my mother struggled to get by, Dad's girlfriend just walked into his life and had everything handed to her on a silver platter. My father also pushed us on her. As children, you often don't have a choice in selecting a parent's new partner (much like you didn't have a choice in the divorce).

By the time "Miss(ed) Opportunity" walked down the aisle with my father, my frustration and fury were boiling over. If getting married wasn't my dad's first mistake, handing out birdseed for the post-nuptial tradition of wishing them well most definitely was. As he and his new bride exited the reception, there we all were, birdseed in hand. Like a pitcher aiming for the perfect strike, I wound up and released, again and again. There were so many people there, she would never know that I was the one whipping the tiny kernels directly at her face. Right? When it hit her square between the eyes, I pointed to the birds.

As this memory washed over me, I found myself in a state of panic fused with PTSD. I told George that we couldn't have a wedding. One of our five children might surely want to pelt one or both of us. Note to self: no birdseed at the wedding.

THE DECISION TO DISSOLVE YOUR MARRIAGE OR TO GET MARRIED AGAIN IS NEVER GOING TO BE AN EASY ONE.

No matter what the $500 divorce billboards might tell you, ending a marriage and daring to begin a new one will not be cheap, nor will it be easy. Even if you are the one to initiate the dissolution, you will carry the weight of convincing yourself, your kids, family, and community that the decision you made was okay. Some of the people around you will be happy for you, some will be sad for you, and some will ceaselessly say they're sorry.

If you watch the first episode of the 2021 HBO series *Scenes from a Marriage* (an adaptation of Ingmar Bergman's 1973 Swedish TV miniseries about a marriage falling apart) you will learn how f*ed-up a marriage can be in a very real way.[23] When I ended things with Mr. Former, I noticed many people were far more unhappy in their relationships than they ever let on. Friends, family, colleagues, strangers. I started to wonder if I would just be trading his crap for someone else's crap after I split. Was that the way love goes? You end your relationship, ride the roller coaster of freedom and grief, and then strap in to do it all over again? Oh, hell no!

As I stuck with my decision to leave my marriage to Mr. Former and endured the emotional ups and downs of the divorce process, I learned far more than I ever had practicing family law. After twentysomething years of being a divorce lawyer, my perception immediately shifted. I felt the things clients didn't tell me (such as what was going on in their brains and hearts).

If you make the decision to leave your marriage, you'll have to summon the courage to follow through without questioning yourself and what you've done. You will inevitably ride the guilt train, but remember to set a clear exit route for yourself before you enter that tunnel of darkness. If you no longer want to be married, you will find something wrong with your partner and your marriage. You may struggle through those feelings and second-guess yourself a hundred times, but don't feel guilty about it if that choice is right for you. Gather your support system, therapist, and journals by the boxload. They will help you find your way.

The healthiest first step will always be to accept the change and be kind to yourself. Attempting to understand it can be too frustrating (especially when the great period of "stuckness" has rushed in and nothing is moving forward). Acceptance is often the best first option. Remember the reasons why you made the choice(s) you did and all the benefits they represented when you weighed the pros and cons. Then, when you reach the point of being able to take action, breathe, and be empowered. You are not alone. Lift your head out of the sand and remember that hope is not a strategy. Advancement takes action. Make the necessary decision and work to understand what comes next. That means knowing the process because you've taken to heart what is in this book.

If you need a little extra encouragement, think about what former wrestler Ronda Rousey would say. Known best for her time in the UFC and WWE and as a professional mixed martial arts fighter, she would likely remind you *not* to be a "Do Nothing Bitch'" (a term she coined to describe someone with zero accountability—someone who only wants to be taken care of). Choose either to work at your marriage or work out what your life will look like if you end things. But whatever you do, *do something*. And if you ultimately choose divorce, work to create a compassionate one.[24]

Redefining the Road Ahead

One day Stella (my '66 convertible Corvette) and I swung by the gas station to fill her up. There was a man on one side of me and a woman on the other. The man came over and asked to take a picture of Stella because his son would love to see it. Then the woman came over and said, "Oh, my gosh, I'd love to have this car." I asked her why she didn't. I noticed she drove a Volvo SUV, so I told her that I also had a "mom SUV" at home! I asked what was stopping her from having both (I knew where she lived, which told me that money was not likely an issue). Her response was, "You're a mom?"

I felt the impact of that moment and her awakening to the fact that having a Stella in her life (literally or metaphorically) would bring her so much happiness. She could choose to have the best of both worlds: a practical mom SUV and her own vintage beauty.

YOUR PAST IS SUPPOSED TO SHAPE YOU, BUT IT DOESN'T HAVE TO DEFINE YOU.

The path you have taken up to now has shaped you, but it does not have to define you. Brené Brown's contribution to personal success in *Rising Strong* hits home for me when she writes, "The irony is that we attempt to disown our difficult stories to appear more whole or more acceptable, but our wholeness—even our wholeheartedness—actually depends on the integration of all of our experiences, including the falls."[25]

Good things can come from bad situations, and you can have what your heart desires. The message I convey to my boys all the time is that *you are the only one in your way of what you want.* You get to choose wherever you go from here. Remember that success, from a personal perspective, is how you define things for yourself. My marriage started to end after I started to question and redefine what success looked like. Now, as a forty-six-year-old mother, business owner, and lawyer, I'm still not sure I know what success ultimately means. Honing that definition is part of the journey. It evolves as you evolve.

Vulnerability appreciates vulnerability. When you are courageous enough to leap directly toward your happiness, share the story of your quest to get there and be real about it. There is a strong chance that the person receiving your words has experienced something similar but didn't have the courage to say it aloud. Your narrative counts. Your narrative can inspire. It will also help you through your own process. Personally, sharing my many wild divorce stories has helped some feel confident enough to make the choice to end their marriage. It has also helped others realize that they want to work harder to stay together. After hearing about all the crazy shit I went through, they were more than happy to try again (with greater effort) to make things right! You go guys and girls! Be that "Do Something Bitch"!

Today is the first day of the rest of your life. Go forth and be fierce in love. Make the empowered choices to shape your own story of happiness and personal success (however you define it). Pursue it and share it courageously. And if you find yourself listening to someone else's divorce story, please, please, please don't say you're sorry!

Glossary of Simplified Legal Speak

LET'S TALK LAW in simplified terms. Here, in plain English, are some of the legal terms referenced in this book. They are divided into four sections: marriage, separation, divorce, and custody.

Marriage

Case law: "Case law" is the interpretation of the statutes (the governing laws) using past cases. The statutes result from legislation, but many times it is unclear what legal principles exist. Therefore, the cases that were heard after the legislation was established serve to better define how to apply the law. In addition, as social changes occur (e.g., marriage equality), the case law allows judges to interpret and clarify the statute.

Couple's Counseling: "Couple's counseling" is working with a licensed marriage and family therapist as you (the couple) work to identify/process issues and address obstacles that may be interfering with the health of the relationship. Contrary to popular belief, couple's counseling is not the beginning of the end of your marriage. Many couples make the mistake of using counseling only when the marriage is hanging together by a thread. Instead, use it at any point to help strengthen your relationship.

Individual Counseling: "Individual counseling" is when you or your spouse work independently with a licensed therapist to identify and process your life story and how it impacts current relationships. There are different types of therapists based on the need of the person seeking aid. Psychologists are often used as counselors or therapists.

Joint Account: A "joint account" is a bank account titled in more than one name. This is different than having an additional user on the account, which can be easily modified by the account holder. A joint account means each of you has equal rights to the account, the monies therein, and you can't close the account without the other party's consent.

Parentification: "'Parentification" refers to behavior through which children are assigned the role of an adult, taking on both emotional and functional responsibilities that typically are performed by the parent. The parent, in turn, takes the dependent position of the child in the parent-child relationship.[26]

Psychiatrist: A "psychiatrist" is a physician who specializes in the diagnosis and treatment of mental illness. Unlike psychologists, these physicians are medical doctors who can prescribe medications. Though they may also use a therapist's techniques, their focus is on prescribing medication as an intervention. Their sessions are also typically shorter than those of psychologists.

Psychologist: A "psychologist" holds a doctorate degree (or several), but they are not physicians (and they cannot prescribe medications in most states). They treat mental health through oral communications and behavior, and are often referred to as "therapists" and "counselors."

Retirement Savings: Several types of accounts can be considered savings for retirement, but "retirement savings" most often refer to accounts that provide tax advantages. Examples of retirement accounts include 401(k), IRAs (Roth or traditional), and 403(b). Note of caution: don't be confused by the nicknames assigned to accounts. For instance, you may have a bank account labeled "tax account" but this is *not* a retirement account; it's a checking or savings account containing funds earmarked for making tax payments.

Separation

Technically speaking, the term "separation" refers to when you and your spouse no longer live under the same roof and one of you has the intention of no longer being married. Depending on your State, legal separation may or may not require you and your spouse to have a contract or Court order. The obvious consequence of separation is that at some point (ranging from sixty days in some States to several years in others), you can legally divorce.

Here are some separation-related terms and what they mean:

Glossary of Simplified Legal Speak

Adultery: In layman's terms "adultery" is also known as "cheating." Legally speaking, adultery is described as a type of marital misconduct that occurs during the marriage and prior to the parties' separation. (BTW, other types of marital misconduct may include abandonment, abuse, reckless spending, or excessive use of alcohol or drugs.) The definition of adultery varies by State. (For example, in North Carolina adultery is actually considered "illicit sexual behavior" and is not limited to sexual intercourse.)

In some States, committing adultery may do nothing more than prevent you from receiving alimony. Depending on your State, it may *not* even fuel grounds for divorce and often will become nothing more than a highlighted detail in the divorce trial to show that the other person was not a committed human during your marriage (which is an emotional argument but not a legal one). Depending on the weight of the evidence, there are instances when evidence of adultery may help to increase the amount or duration of the alimony term.

Discovery: "Discovery" is a legal term and short for the discovery process, or the exchange of information to support the claims each party has filed. It is the procedure during which each party in a lawsuit (including divorce actions) can obtain (discover) evidence from the other or from third parties. In domestic cases, it is nearly impossible to admit evidence that has not been supplied to the other party in advance of the trial if discovery has been completed (so you can blow out that smoking gun if it's found anytime after that). Discovery can come in many shapes and sizes, including inter-rogatories (a set number of questions), a Request for Production of Documents, a Request for Admissions, a subpoena, or even the deposition of a party or witness. Because the information gleaned from the discovery process is used by each party to develop a strategy for the case, there should be time after discovery to prepare properly for Court, mediation, or arbitration.

Divorce Attorney: "Divorce attorney" and "family law attorney" are interchangeable terms. (On a bad day, I say that I'm a divorce attorney. On a good day, I'm a family law attorney.) The term "domestic attorney" may also be used to define a lawyer certified to help you through a marital or divorce case.

In divorce, a good divorce attorney will care about how things are going to be divided between you and your spouse, what financial support is going to exist, and where the kids will put their heads on a pillow every night.

Divorce

Divorce is either the last thing that happens or something that happens along the way after deciding to dissolve your marriage. Among other things, the legal consequence of divorce is that you are free to marry again. Despite misconceptions, divorce *doesn't* automatically resolve the other issues that stem from your relationship, including how property is divided, what financial support is paid or received (alimony), parenting time with the children (custody), financial support for your children (child support), or whether you are required to pay or be reimbursed attorney fees.

Here are some divorce-related terms and what they mean:

Alienation of Affection: "Alienation of affection" is a (controversial) lawsuit brought by a married (or formerly married) person who claims that the actions of a third party deprived them of the love and affection of their spouse. Hawaii, Mississippi, New Mexico, North Carolina, South Dakota, and Utah are the only States that still recognize Alienation of Affection.[27] If you are in one of these six States and looking to take on a claim, you had better be prepared to prove that (1) you and your spouse were married and a genuine love and affection existed between you, (2) that love and affection was alienated and destroyed, and (3) the wrongful and malicious acts of the third party alienated the affection of the plaintiff's spouse.

Alimony: "Alimony" is the support paid to an ex-spouse (its terms cover how much, how long, and what can trigger its termination). You will want to know if your State has an alimony calculator. If so, note that even when there are calculators, what has been established through statute may not always fit a person's specific circumstances. In most States, alimony will come down to whether there is enough money to go around.

Alternative Dispute Resolution: "Alternative Dispute Resolution," also known as ADR, refers to the method by which you have chosen to resolve your divorce. You need to determine your resolution process ahead of time (whether it be mediation, arbitration, or litigation) so that both parties can prepare accordingly.

Arbitration: On the one hand, "arbitration" is like mediation because it uses a neutral third party to help reach resolution; on the other hand arbitration proceedings work very much like Courtroom proceedings (though they typically occur in a boardroom setting). You go through the discovery process (the exchanging of evidence) and allow an arbitrator to receive your testimony. The arbitrator (a lawyer) then makes the final decision (the Arbitrator's Award). If you don't like what was decided, you can appeal.

Arbitrator's Award: After the arbitrator hears all the evidence presented, the arbitrator provides a ruling or decision, often referred to as the Arbitrator's Award.

Dissolution of Marriage: "Dissolution of marriage" is interchangeable with the term "divorce." Divorce is the legal termination of your legal marriage.

Lawsuit: The term "lawsuit" is interchangeable with

the term "complaint." It is the start of litigation, which means that the case is going to be decided by a judge, unless it is resolved in advance by agreement between the parties.

Litigation: "Litigation" is a court proceeding to dissolve a marriage (and a very expensive story time), whereby a judge makes the ultimate decisions after both parties have had a chance to state their case. You have no choice in how long these proceedings will be or whether you accept the final decision.

Mediation: In "mediation" a neutral party known as a "mediator" (who is often, but not always, an attorney who practices family law) follows a typical procedure to help you find agreement on the issues in conflict (aka, the "settlement"). Most divorcing couples are required to attend mediation as an alternative form of resolution before taking the case to court. For some, it becomes a primary resolution choice.

Verified Pleading: A "verified pleading" is a formal statement of a claim that is often filed with the Court after you have affirmed it in front of a notary.

Custody

"Custody" may also be referred to as "visitation." The "custody schedule" or "visitation schedule" may also be referred to as the "parenting schedule." Ultimately, it is where the children lay their heads to rest at night. Custody is broken down into two parts: "physical custody" and "legal custody." Physical custody refers to the parenting schedule. Legal custody refers to how and who makes major decisions for the children, such as medical and academic decisions. Whether they have pancakes for breakfast is up to the parent who has the children in their care when breakfast is served.

Here are other custody-related terms:

Best-Interests Standard: The "best-interests standard" is the standard that the Court will use to determine custody of a child. Factors that assist the Court making a determination about welfare and best interests include the physical, mental, and/or financial fitness of a parent (or person seeking custody or visitation) and any other considerations brought out by the evidence and relevant to the child's welfare.

Child Support: "Child support" is the support paid by one parent to the other to cover expenses related to your child or children.

Child Support Calculator: Child support is calculated using presumptive guidelines mandated by statute. The Court uses these guidelines to determine an amount of child support that is reasonable considering the incomes of both parents and the needs of the children. Child support calculators are *not* the same in every state.

Co-Parenting: "Co-parenting" is an opportunity for children of divorce to have equal access to both parents. Finding the methods, schedules, and solutions that are the best fit for you and your family may include the use of virtual apps or calendars, guidance from a certified parenting coordinator, or support from a family counselor or therapist.

Joint Legal Custody: "Legal custody" refers to the ability to make decisions (usually medical and academic) for your child. "Joint legal custody" means you and the other parent share these responsibilities. Day-to-day decisions are left to the parent who has physical custody of the child at the time.

Supervised Visits: The term "visitation" is interchange-able with "custody." In a case of "supervised visits," an allegation leads the Court to determine that a child's visits with a parent should be supervised. From there, it must be determined who the supervisor will be and how their observations will be documented.

Tender Years Doctrine: The "Tender Years Doctrine" has been a legal principle in family law since the late nineteenth century. It presumes that during a child's "tender" years (generally regarded as under four years of age), the mother should have custody of the child. The doctrine has been abolished but many believe the principle is still followed in theory.

Notes

CHAPTER 2

1. Some statutes allow for the party alleging domestic violence to also seek temporary custody and exclusive use of the parties' residence as additional awards. Often, allegations of drug use are included in those claims. Unfortunately, fabricating or embellishing facts to win a custody case or gain possession of a home numbs the judges hearing such matters. To make things worse, even if the allegations are fabricated or embellished, the "victim" may begin to believe the allegations that were handcrafted by counsel or created by narrative, ultimately creating a war that will likely never be undone. The children suffer. Your family will likely never heal. And sadly, the Courts begin to question the validity of real claims with real victims. Don't abuse the system.

PART 1

2. Steven Stosny, Ph.D., "Realize Your Core Value," *Psychology Today,* June 21, 2020, https://www.psychologytoday.com/us/blog/anger-in-the-age-entitlement/202006/realize-your-core-value.

CHAPTER 3

3. Esther Perel, "An Exercise in Adaptability: How to Bend Without Breaking," Letters from Esther, October 13, 2021, YouTube video, 2:04, https://www.youtube.com/watch?v=_NpuJsh8c9I.

CHAPTER 5

4. Dr. Marni Feuerman, "Managing vs. Resolving Conflict in Relationships: The Blueprints for Success," Gottman Institute, November 9, 2017, https://www.gottman.com/blog/managing-vs-resolving-conflict-relationships-blueprints-success/.

5. Dr. Harriet Lerner, "I'm Sorry: How to Apologize and Why It Matters, Part 1 of 2," interview with Brené Brown, May 6, 2020, in *Unlocking Us,* podcast, MP3 audio, 8:30, https://brenebrown.com/podcast/harriet-lerner-and-brene-im-sorry-how-to-apologize-why-it-matters-part-1-of-2/.

Notes

6. For the record, based on your respective State, it is not uncommon to plead the Fifth in civil action.

7. Wendy Wang, "Who Cheats More? The Demographics of Infidelity in America," The Institute for Family Studies, January 10, 2018, https://ifstudies.org/blog/who-cheats-more-the-demographics-of-cheating-in-america.

8. Dr. Alexandra H. Solomon, "Once a Cheater, Always a Cheater? How to Tell if the Person You're Dating May Be a Perpetual Cheater," *Psychology Today,* October 26, 2020, https://www.psychologytoday.com/us/blog/loving-bravely/202010/once-cheater-always-cheater.

9. CDC/NCHS National Vital Statistics System, "Provisional Number of Divorces and Annulments and Rate: United States, 2000–2019," PDF, 2, https://www.cdc.gov/nchs/data/dvs/national-marriage-divorce-rates-00-19.pdf.

CHAPTER 7

10. Glennon Doyle, *Untamed* (The Dial Press, 2020) 60.

11. All State-separation-period references are as of time of writing and subject to change.

CHAPTER 9

12. Jennifer A. Engelhardt, "The Developmental Implications of Parentification: Effects on Childhood Attachment," *Graduate Student Journal of Psychology* 14 (2012): 45, https://www.tc.columbia.edu/media/centers/gsjp/gsjp-volume-pdfs/25227_Engelhardt_Parentification.pdf.

13. Robert Epstein, "What Makes a Good Parent?," *Scientific American Mind,* November 2010, https://www.scientificamerican.com/article/what-makes-a-good-parent/.

14. Bill Eddy, foreword to Megan Hunter and Andrea LaRochelle, *The High-Conflict Co-Parenting Survival Guide: Reclaim Your Life One Week at a Time* (Scottsdale, AZ: Unhooked Books, 2019).

CHAPTER 11

15. Doyle, *Untamed,* 60.

CHAPTER 12

16. I wasn't alone in these feelings either. In her November 2021 interview with Oprah, global superstar Adele spoke openly about her amicable divorce and said she questioned if things would have been better if she had just kept her mouth shut and carried on. She left the marriage because she wasn't happy, but she hated hurting the two people she loved

Notes

the most in the world (her son and husband). Emily Yahr, "The Four Most Personal Revelations from Oprah's Interview with Adele, from Her Divorce to Weight Loss to New Boyfriend," *The Washington Post*, November 15, 2021, https://www.washingtonpost.com/arts-entertainment/2021/11/15/adele-oprah-interview-concert/.

17. CDC/NCHS, "Provisional Number of Divorces and Annulments and Rate."

CHAPTER 15

18. Zach Johnson, "Blake Shelton Talks Losing Weight on a 'Divorce Diet,'" *E! News*, September 24, 2015, https://www.eonline.com/news/699428/blake-shelton-talks-losing-weight-on-a-divorce-diet.

19. A. Pawlowski, "Divorce Diet: When Slimming Down After Splitting Up Isn't a Good Thing," *TODAY*, August 17, 2016, https://www.today.com/health/divorce-diet-when-slimming-down-after-splitting-isn-t-good-t101857.

20. Jeffery Sobal, Barbara Rauschenbach, and Edward Frongillo, "Marital Status Changes and Body Weight Changes: A US Longitudinal Analysis," *Social Science & Medicine* 56, no. 7 (April 2003):https://doi.org/10.1016/s0277-9536(02)00155-7.

21. Jenna Marie Strizzi et al., "Divorce Is Stressful, But How Stressful? Perceived Stress Among Recently Divorced Danes," *Journal of Divorce & Remarriage* 62, no. 1 (January 2021): https://doi.org/10.1080/10502556.2021.1871838.

CHAPTER 16

22. As an important side note, domestic violence will always be an important point to consider when it comes to staying in or leaving your relationship. Never accept any kind of physical or emotional abuse.

23. A compassionate divorce is a very mature but emotional response to supporting what you want and what someone else wants.

24. Brené Brown, *Rising Strong* (New York: Random House, 2015), 38.

25. Engelhardt, "Developmental Implications of Parentification," 45.

GLOSSARY

26. At time of writing.

Acknowledgments

YOU ARE HOLDING this book because of all the people who pushed me to grow miles beyond the days of saying I was sorry.

My gratitude goes out to:

- Joscelyn, for your endless patience, poise, and professionalism and for always being quick to help me find the words.

- My mother—my biggest fan—for always reminding me that today is the first day of the rest of my life.

- My father, for not letting me forget my purpose.

- Adam and Chris and their families, for showing me extra compassion and just for being my big brothers when I needed an ear.

- Yvonne, for being my one-woman village, for treating my boys as if they are your own, and for lifting us up in prayer.

- Mr. Former, for our beautiful three boys and a lifetime of lessons.

Acknowledgments

- My Firm Family, for your commitment to our clients, our community, and one another.

- Kurt and my Vistage family, for holding me accountable and for elevating my leadership every single day.

- My sisterhood, for brainstorming, drinking wine, and distracting me when I needed it most.

- My clients, for entrusting me and being my teachers as much as I may have been yours.

- George, for being my unexpected light and for showing me the magic of new beginnings.

- Scarlet: may you know you are more than loved. I am so proud of you.

About Nicole Sodoma

SODOMA LAW FOUNDER Nicole Sodoma is a marriage-loving divorce attorney. She is a mom to three boys, a now ex-wife, a soon-to-be new wife, a woman business owner, a lawyer, a friend to many, and a trusted advisor to thousands . . . not always in that particular order.

Packing a powerful punch of wit, care, tenacity, and perspective, Sodoma is a fearless crusader for marriage and divorce education in the often-dreaded field of family law. Over the past twenty-five years, she has been recognized for her steadfast commitment to her clients, her entrepreneurship, her vision, and her community involvement. Quickly rising as a national authority on divorce and family law, her insights have been featured on the *TODAY* show, and in the *Wall Street Journal*, *Business Insider*, the *Washington Post*, *USA Today*, *Women's Health* magazine, *Parents Magazine*, and Care.com.

She is a graduate of Cumberland School of Law at Samford University, a family law litigator, certified parenting coordinator, and certified collaborative law attorney. And for those asking, her '66 white convertible Corvette does indeed have a name. It's Stella. And yes, she got her groove back.

About
Sodoma Law

IN OUR FIRST year together, my ex-husband and I had every intention of starting a family but nothing was happening. I started seeing an OB-GYN named Dr. SUNY ("See You Next Year"). He told me that if I couldn't have children within the next twelve months then I should let him know. Then he patted me on the shoulder and gave me a prescription for Xanax. I quit seeing him faster than the Road Runner trying to outrun Wile E. Coyote.

That month, I got pregnant and later had my first son. Then, following four miscarriages, a ton of fertility drugs, chiropractor visits, acupuncture, and whatever else I could conjure up, we had our second son, our IUI (intrauterine insemination) baby. Then came bold number ten, our IVF (in vitro fertilization) baby. He was one of thirty-seven embryos. None survived or were healthy except my number-ten embryo—now my third beautiful boy.

If you go to a place and trust someone who is responsible for your mental, emotional, or financial well-being and all you get is a pat on the back and a prescription for anxiety medication, it's not okay.

When I opened the doors of Sodoma Law in 2008, it was with the intention of building a different kind of law firm, with Dr. SUNY top of mind. I focused on creating a culture of a "firm family" that showed commitment to the greatest levels of care for clients, team, and community. I didn't want anyone to feel alone in the divorce process, and I wanted to build a team who would help every client find their way through the hurdles of separation and divorce with empathy and determination, in and out of court. This concept soon became known as "The Sodoma Way," and this practice is who I am.

When clients come to us in the middle of a divorce or custody battle, we believe they deserve that blend of qualities from each of our divorce/

family law attorneys. They need attorneys who will fight for them in the courtroom and empower them to achieve their personal goals at a difficult time in their lives. Each of our attorneys and staff members believes not only in their ability to make a difference in a client's life but also in their ability to support the clients' emotional, spiritual, and physical well-being.

Sodoma Law grew from two people to twelve in just its first year. Then steadily yet organically, the firm kept expanding, across borders and throughout the intricacies of unique family law circumstances. As of 2021, we have a team of more than twenty lawyers and fifty staff across multiple states, and our clients include everyone from NFL greats to NASCAR wives and neighbors down the road.

All too often lawyers will pat you on the back and tell you that everything is going to be okay, but that's just not the way it's going to be with divorce. My primary goal is to ensure that everyone who comes to work with us feels assured that *they* are going to be okay, because they are. I believe it's our job as family law attorneys to educate our clients on their various legal options to reduce that anxiety and allow them to feel more in control of their cases.

About Sodoma Law

Welcome to a new era of family law. If you're struggling through a divorce or within your marriage, I want you to know that we have either been there or heard it. At Sodoma Law, we dedicate ourselves to being your family law and divorce advocate.

We are in this together.

—Nicole